THE CALIFORNIA PIZZA KITCHEN COOKBOOK

The California Pizza Kitchen Cookbook

By Larry Flax & Rick Rosenfield

Photography by Brian Leatart

Macmillan • USA

MACMILLAN

A Simon & Schuster Macmillan Company
1633 Broadway
New York, NY 10019

Contact Library of Congress for full Cataloging-in-Publication Data.

ISBN: 0-02-860988-3

Manufactured in the United States of America

10 9 8 7 6 5 4 3 2 1

Design by Amy Peppler Adams—designLab, Seattle
Food styling by Karen Gillingham
Prop styling by Kim Wong
For a list of credits for props, see page 90.

Dedication

To my parents, Rose and Bill, and to my sister and brother-in-law, Linda and Bob, for always believing in me no matter what path I followed; to my wife, Joan, for taking my hand as we walk this path; and to Peter, whose exploration of the future awaits—always take the risk.

—Larry Flax

To my wife, Esther, who shared the tremendous risk of my transition from lawyer to restaurateur, and gave her heart and soul as CPK's first hostess and whose passion for excellence continues to burn as brightly as ever; to my son, Ian, who started with the first CPK part-time during high school and now, after college, works as our highly valued Director of Quality Control; and to my daughters Nicole and Dana, who share all our pride in being part of CPK's extended family.

—Rick Rosenfield

Acknowledgments

We have more than 6,000 CPK employees who lend their energies daily to our restaurants throughout the country and serve our customers splendidly.

We express a special acknowledgment to Gary Beauregard, our Vice President of Research and Development, who has joined us throughout the years in developing and refining the CPK recipes. His efforts in adapting our recipes for the home kitchen have allowed the creation of this book.

We also wish to extend special thanks to Sarah Goldsmith, CPK's Vice President of Public Relations, for her tireless effort in putting this book together. Without Sarah's constant "nudging" this project would probably forever have remained on the back burner.

Contents

Preface

Recipe for Success

Looking back over the eleven years and more than 80 restaurants that have passed since we opened the very first California Pizza Kitchen, we realize that much of our success goes beyond serving great food. It is due to the relationships we have with our customers, employees, and their communities; and to our devotion to giving back to those who support us. In addition to working with charities in every city where we have opened a restaurant, we have supported organizations like the Starlight Foundation, SHARE, Pediatric AIDS, Make-A-Wish, Juvenile Diabetes, the American Heart Association and Child Help.

Although charitable giving has always been one of our highest priorities, now it is even more of one. Our royalties from the sales of this cookbook will be distributed to charities nationwide. It is only because of this wonderful opportunity to benefit worthy causes, that after years of requests for our recipes, we have finally decided to make available our secrets.

L. S. Flax   *Rick Rosenfield*

Our World on a Pizza

A Brief Introduction

In the beginning, there was duck sausage. And goat cheese. And BBQ chicken, thank goodness. Later, we added Thai chicken, BLT and tandoori. And Peking duck. And then vegetarian. And Moo Shu. And so that purists would feel comfortable, we also offered mushroom, pepperoni, sausage and just plain cheese. Even so, nothing about pizza has been the same since we opened the first California Pizza Kitchen in Beverly Hills in 1985. But that is the point.

As you will discover over the course of making and sampling the easy-to-follow and unique recipes contained in this cookbook, we redefined the traditional concept of pizza not only simply by indulging our own love of food, but by attempting to interpret what Americans love to eat. Our approach reflects the unique, cutting-edge, fun-loving, experimental spirit of California and has led us to create pizzas topped with everything from eggplant to Eggs Benedict.

It is no coincidence that this unpretentious combination of bread, tomato and cheese is more popular than ever. Each year, more than 11 billion slices of pizza are eaten in the United States. The average American consumes almost 25 pounds per year. The best-selling topping, according to the U.S. Department of Agriculture, is pepperoni. But at California Pizza Kitchen—where upwards of 50 million pizzas have been consumed—the clear favorite is BBQ chicken.

Our entry into the business was as nontraditional as our BBQ chicken pizza. As one-time federal prosecutors and later as law partners specializing in criminal defense, we traveled frequently and were exposed to a variety of great food and wine, which kindled our interest in starting a restaurant. In 1984, we began leaning toward Italian food because, like everyone else, we recognized it as a hearty and healthy cuisine. Italian food was no longer viewed as simple, filling starches but as beneficial complex carbohydrates. We visited several cafe-teria-style pasta bars, including one such place at a local shopping mall that kept a thin, rubbery cheese pizza spinning slowly under a heat lamp. We noticed that about half the people ordered pizza, regardless of whether they had pasta, too. We agreed we should do pizza along with pasta.

Later, in the car, we said, "What about the wood-burning pizza oven and the new California-style of pizza that was beginning to develop in San Francisco and Los Angeles?" And at that moment, we knew we had the concept. We would make the oven the centerpiece of the restaurant, arrange the chairs and tables around it like seats in a theater and serve this new style of pizza. But like good lawyers, we decided to do some research.

However, pizza is anything but new. Its invention is credited to the Etruscans and Greeks. As early as 700 B.C., they whipped up rounded, flat bread baked under hot stones and topped it with a zesty mix of oils, olives, garlic and onions. Not a tomato in sight. About 2,000 years later—after the first tomatoes were imported to Italy from America—the Neapolitans added tomato to their pizza. And in 1889, celebrated chef Don Raffaele Esposito, of Naples, honored Queen Margherita with a special pizza topped in the colors of the Italian flag—tomato, basil and, for the first time, white mozzarella cheese!

In 1905, America's first pizzeria opened in lower New York City. After World War II, pizza

Deep Dish: *Actress Jane Seymour helps Rick and Larry celebrate California Pizza Kitchen's opening in Chicago*

parlors spread across the country as soldiers who had served in Italy and acquired a taste for the savory and satisfying food returned home and created instant demand. By the 1960s, New York, Chicago and Boston all had their own unique variations—thin crust, deep dish and so on.

Inevitably the West Coast checked in with its own version. In the late 1970s, the very talented San Francisco chef Jeremiah Tower, who has since opened Stars but then cooked for Alice Waters at her famed Berkeley restaurant Chez Panisse, dropped goat cheese and other delicacies on a thin, individual-sized crust, cooked it in a wood-burning oven reminiscent of the Greeks and gave birth to California-style pizza. Wolfgang Puck nudged it a step farther by adding duck sausage and combinations of exotic cheeses when he opened Spago in Los Angeles.

Our goal was to take these gourmet pizzas out of expensive restaurants that catered to the rich and famous and make them easily available to the public. Our next task was choosing a location. We selected an unlikely site in Beverly Hills, where three restaurants had previously failed. But we loved it. Choosing a name was quite challenging. Then Larry woke up at 3:00 a.m. with a name. He managed to wait a few hours before calling Rick. Soon after, we had our first and only breakfast meeting. "I've got the name—California Pizza Kitchen," said Larry, barely able to contain his excitement. Rick mulled the name over. "Isn't

A Sure Bet: *Former heavyweight champ Evander Hollyfield and baseball great Steve Garvey ensured CPK would be a winner in Las Vegas.*

that a little pedestrian for Beverly Hills?" he asked. (We had been thinking of Italian-esque names like *Primavera* and *Ciao*.) "Listen," said Larry, "if we don't name it California Pizza Kitchen, you're going to be really sick when someone else does." Right away, Rick agreed that he was right.

However, further market research was needed. That night we had dinner with some friends who were entertaining relatives from Rhode Island, and we asked their opinion of the different names we were considering. More importantly, we asked which one they would be most likely to go to. They selected California Pizza Kitchen. The others, they explained, sounded like any other Italian restaurant; but they would eat at California Pizza Kitchen, they said, "just to see what you

Going Bicoastal: *At the opening in New York City, Rick and Larry advised Dr. Ruth Westheimer what to order, and it was good for her.*

a professional chef hired as a consultant. From the very first day, we observed that our customers had little interest in exotic sausage pizzas. However, the BBQ chicken drove them absolutely crazy. It was a smash. Even people who claimed to not like pizza said, "I love this."

That opened our eyes. With our consultant gone, we started experimenting with all sorts of new, exciting and nontraditional combinations of toppings we had dreamed about putting on pizza but didn't dare—until then. We then created the BLT, Thai chicken and even egg salad pizza. Countless others popped into our heads. Encouraged and confident, we decided to let our own taste buds guide us and simply top our pizzas with the food Americans like to eat most, which includes just about everything—Japanese, French, Indian, Italian, Mexican, Southwestern, Cajun, vegetarian and so on. In other words, we realized that we could put the entire world on a pizza.

And that's what we did. Today, we like to say, "There are fourteen ethnically diverse cultures peacefully coexisting on a thin delicious crust."

Like a melting pot of cultures, our menu reflects popular tastes and trends as they surface throughout the country. Cajun cooking, for instance, was the rage when we opened in 1985. Everything was blackened. Our Cajun pizza was instantly among the best selling pizzas we served. As the popularity of Cajun food declined, the pizza sank to the bottom ten percent, and we retired it from the menu. In its

flakes from out there are up to." And that was our market research.

Our first menu, which included traditional pizza like mushroom, pepperoni and sausage with tomato sauce also featured duck, rabbit and lamb sausage pizzas, as well as the original BBQ chicken pizza, was designed for us by place, we developed the rosemary chicken and potato pizza to meet the craze for rotisserie chicken and roasted potatoes, and as soon as we added it to the menu, it soared to the top. Similarly, one of our early favorites, the duck sausage pizza, is gone as are some others. In their place we've added pizzas such as Santa Fe Chicken, Chicken Dijon, Tostada, and Eggplant Parmesan, which have soared to the top of the charts.

We hope that by using this cookbook you will be similarly inspired to try some of our all-time favorite pizzas and also invent some new favorites of your own. Having expanded into major pizza cities like Chicago, Boston and New York, we have found that our style of California pizza transcends regional boundaries. We are justifiably proud that California Pizza has taken its rightful place on the national pizza map.

Do not be afraid to let yourself dream. We did, and look what happened. It is our hope that this book defines for you this new phenomenon called California pizza.

The Big Cheese: Entertainment mogul Merv Griffin joined his friends Rick and Larry in bringing California pizza to Atlantic City.

Taste, Fun, Variety:

The CPK Guide to

Making Pizza at Home

Long before we opened the first California Pizza Kitchen, we made pizzas at home. We did not have wood-burning ovens like we do at our restaurants. They are great for restaurants because they cook fast and impart a wonderful flavor, but you do not need them to make truly great pizzas at home.

At first, we set pizza cookbooks on the kitchen counter and tried our hand at plain cheese pizza. Then we added basil, peppers and assorted fresh ingredients, working up to what we thought were adventurous pizzas like BBQ chicken and BLT. Eventually, through our own trials and tastings, we concluded that anything that tastes great on bread will taste even better on pizza, and that has proved true with few exceptions.

Once, we spent the day experimenting at the Beverly Hills restaurant and concocted a truly unexpected creation—a cheeseburger pizza. Really. We had put dollops of hamburger meat on a crust and surrounded them with tomato, cheddar cheese and sliced lettuce after taking it out of the oven. It tasted great, but quickly our excitement waned. Unfortunately, it made us want a thick cheeseburger rather than a pizza. That is why we have never put it on the menu.

But many of our other experiments have proved some of California Pizza Kitchen's biggest hits. We came up with our chicken teriyaki pizza on a dare from a reporter who refused to believe we could invent a great-tasting pizza right in front of him at home. We created our Thai chicken, tostada, vegetarian, shrimp scampi and Moo Shu pizzas by observing what we and our friends ordered at restaurants, trying them on a pizza and discovering they were delicious. You can do the same in your kitchen at home.

Use our earliest days as inspiration. They show that the possibilities for creating new, previously unimaginable combinations are unlimited. Once, we whipped up an Eggs Benedict pizza for brunch. We also came up with our version of an omelet by topping a pizza crust with eggs scrambled with mushroom, pepperoni and sausage. And our Thai Chicken pizza hooked people on first bite.

As for disasters, we always mention the egg salad pizza, though in truth whenever fresh, old-fashioned egg salad was spread over a warm crust just out of the oven, it was irresistible. If not for the fear of high cholesterol, it might still be on the menu today. The only outright failure was the chili dog pizza. It bombed (though we still offer it around World Series time). Good pizza, though.

And that is the point. If you are going to make pizza at home, your guidelines should be the same as ours—taste, fun and variety. Think about what foods you love. Have you tried them in different combinations? Use your imagination. Beyond that, we have a few tips:

● Keep things simple. More isn't always better.

● Don't overdo the ingredients. Aim for one representative taste from each of the elements in every bite.

● Be mindful of what the oven is going to do to your pizza. Do you need to precook some ingredients and not others? The final cooking should bring everything to the ultimate state of taste perfection.

● And finally, don't worry, have fun!

The worst that can happen is that you will throw out a pizza. No big deal (after all, it's not a steak). But at best, you will amaze yourself and eat something unique and wonderful, something that you created. As we always say, "If it sounds like it will taste good on pizza, you have a ninety-nine percent chance of being right."

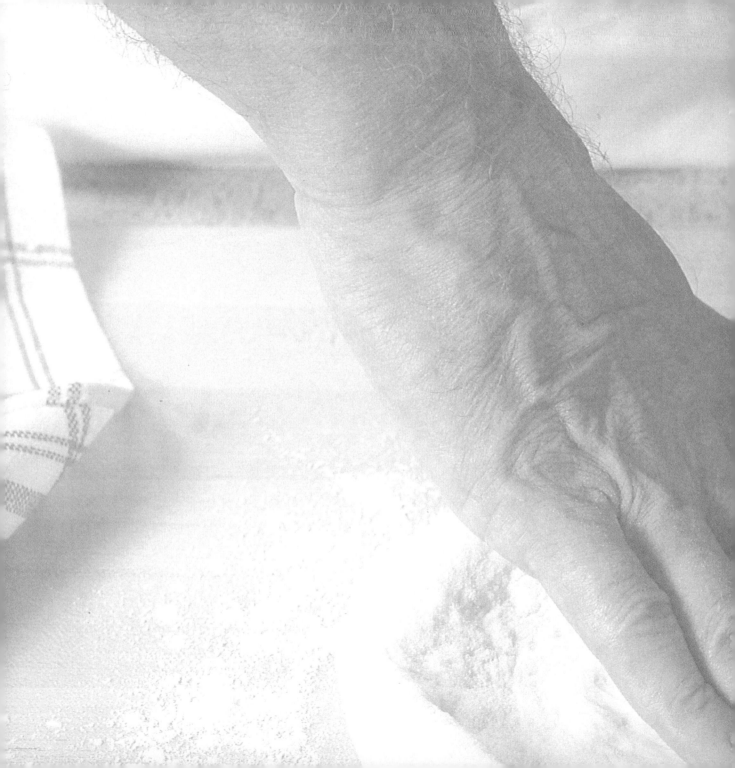

The Case for
Great Dough

Perhaps no element of a pizza is as controversial as the crust, but leave it to former lawyers to settle the case. We believe a good crust should be hearty, flavorful, chewy, strong and rich; we are providing the dough recipes for two such delicious examples—our standard pizza crust and a special honey-wheat crust.

No matter which one you choose to make, preparation should really start the day before you plan to serve the pizza. Do not panic, though. Making wonderful dough does not take as much time as it sounds. In fact, the dough actually works harder than you—the yeast develops and digests the starches in the flour, while the dough ferments, proofs and readies itself to be rolled, shaped, topped, baked and consumed.

Basically, flour has two main elements, starch and gluten. Our dough is made from a high-gluten flour. *Gluten*, a form of protein found in some of the harder winter wheats, is what gives dough its chewy quality. High-gluten bread flours are available in most grocery stores.

After mixing the ingredients together, we recommend allowing the dough to rise three times. First, let it rise at room temperature until it doubles in bulk; then punch down the dough ball and put it in the refrigerator. When it has risen again, divide it in two equal pieces (or four if making appetizer pizzas) and let those rise at room temperature until they double in bulk. At this point, the dough should be soft, puffy, slightly warm to touch and ready to go.

You can either flour the dough liberally and roll it out on a nonporous surface with a rolling pin, or you can make it like we do at our restaurants by either hand stretching or twirling the dough. If you choose the second option, we suggest making more dough than you intend to use, especially the first time out.

Then you can twirl with confidence. If you drop the dough or if the family pooch intercepts it like a Frisbee, no big deal. You still have more to fall back on.

Of course, if pizza is a last-minute decision, and you are strapped for time, you can use the dough after the first rising, as outlined in the recipe that follows, or you can certainly make a delicious pizza using a ready-made, store-bought dough. Remember, great artists paint masterpieces on all types of surfaces, not only canvas.

Pizza Dough

MAKES DOUGH FOR 2 9-INCH PIZZAS

Basic Pizza Dough

1 teaspoon yeast
$^1/_2$ cup plus 1 tablespoon warm water (105° to 110°F)
1$^1/_2$ cups bread flour or all-purpose flour
2 teaspoons sugar
1 teaspoon salt
1 tablespoon extra virgin olive oil plus 1 teaspoon for coating

Honey-Wheat Pizza Dough

1 teaspoon yeast
$^1/_2$ cup plus 1 teaspoon warm water (105° to 110°F)
1 cup bread flour
$^1/_2$ cup whole wheat flour
5 teaspoons clover honey
1 teaspoon salt
1 tablespoon extra virgin olive oil plus 1 teaspoon for coating

Note: The mixing and handling of the two types of dough are essentially identical except that the honey-wheat tends to rise more slowly.

To make the dough:

❶ Dissolve the yeast in the water and set aside for 5 to 10 minutes. Be sure that the water is not hot; temperatures of 120°F and above will kill the yeast, and your dough will not rise.

❷ **If using an upright electric mixer,** such as a KitchenAid®, use the mixing paddle attachment because the batch size is too small for the dough hook to be effective. Combine all other ingredients (except the additional teaspoon olive oil) and combine them with the dissolved yeast in the mixing bowl. (Do not pour the salt directly into the yeast water because this would kill some of the yeast.) Allow these 2 ingredients to mix gradually; use the lowest 2 speeds to mix the dough. Mix for 2 to 3 minutes, until the dough is smooth and elastic. Overmixing will produce tough, rubbery dough, and friction will cause dough to rise too fast.

If using a food processor, use a dough "blade" made of plastic rather than the sharp steel knife attachment, which would cut the gluten strands and ruin the consistency of the dough. Otherwise, proceed as above (step 2). Be especially cautious not to mix too long with a food processor because the temperature resulting from the friction of mixing could easily exceed 120°F, killing your yeast. Mix only until a smooth dough ball is formed.

If mixing by hand, place the dry ingredients in a 4- to 6-quart mixing bowl; make a well in the middle and pour in the liquids (reserving the teaspoon of olive oil). Use a wooden spoon to combine the ingredients. Once initial mixing is done, you can lightly oil your hands and begin kneading the dough; knead for 5 minutes. When done the dough should be slightly tacky (that is, it should be barely beyond sticking to your hands).

3 Lightly oil the dough ball and the interior of a 1-quart glass bowl. Place the dough ball in the bowl and seal the bowl with clear food wrap; seal air tight. Set aside at room temperature (70–80°) to rise until double in bulk; about 1½ to 2 hours.

4 (The dough could be used at this point, but it will not be that wonderful, chewy, flavorful dough that it will later become.) Punch down the dough, re-form a nice round ball and return it to the same bowl; cover again with clear food wrap. Place the bowl in the refrigerator overnight, covered airtight.

5 About 2 hours before you are ready to assemble your pizza, remove the dough from the refrigerator. Use a sharp knife to divide the dough into 2 equal portions (or 4 equal portions if making appetizer-sized pizza or if smaller, 6-inch pizzas are desired).

6 Roll the smaller doughs into round balls on a smooth, clean surface; be sure to seal any holes by pinching or rolling.

7 Place the newly formed dough balls in a glass casserole dish, spaced far enough apart to allow for each to double in size. Seal the top of the dish air-tight with clear food wrap. Set aside at room temperature until the dough balls have doubled in size (about 2 hours). They should be smooth and puffy.

To stretch and form the dough for pizza:

1 Sprinkle a medium dusting of flour over a 12x12-inch clean, smooth surface. Use a metal spatula or dough scraper to carefully remove a dough ball from the glass casserole dish, being very careful to preserve its round shape. Flour the dough liberally. Place the floured dough on the floured smooth surface.

2 Use your hand or a rolling pin to press the dough down forming a flat circle about 1/2 inch thick. Pinch the dough between your fingers all around the edge of circle, forming a lip or rim that rises about 1/4 inch above the center surface of the dough. You may continue this outward stretching motion of the hands until you have reached a 9-inch diameter pizza dough. Or, for the more adventurous, proceed to step 3.

3 Here comes the tricky part: Place the rimmed dough on the backs of your hands with your fingers spread about an inch apart. The edge of the dough should rest on the backs of your second knuckles of both hands.

❹ Wind up for the toss by rotating your hands ¼ revolution in the opposite direction from the way you will be spinning the dough.

To wind up: Both hands align with your chin; your hands turn so that your right hand is the farthest away with palm facing (thumb up). Your left hand should be closer to you with the thumb down.

❺ Stretch the dough out slightly and spin the dough upward by flicking your hands outward in opposite directions. The motion is like both hands are quickly losing an arm wrestling match. Your left hand arcs up and out to the left at the same time your right hand arcs up and out to the right. Catch the spinning dough on the backs of your hands. (Or pick it up off the floor and try again—just kidding!) If necessary, reposition your hands and repeat the toss until you've formed a 9-inch circular dough.

To dress the pizza:

❶ Lightly sprinkle cornmeal, semolina or flour over the surface of a wooden pizza peel. Arrange the stretched dough over the floured peel surface. Work quickly (following one of the pizza recipes) to dress the pizza so that the dough won't become soggy or sticky from sauces and toppings.

❷ When you are ready to transfer the pizza to the pizza stone in the preheated oven, grasp the handle of the peel and execute a very small test jerk to verify that the pizza will come easily off the peel. If the dough doesn't move freely, carefully lift the edges of the dough and try to rotate it by hand. Extreme cases may require that you toss more flour under the dough edges.

Once the dough is moving easily on the peel, open the oven and position the edge of the peel over the center of the stone about ⅔ from the front of the stone.* Jiggle and tilt the peel to get the pizza to start sliding off. When the pizza begins to touch the stone, pull the peel quickly out from under it. Don't attempt to move the pizza until it has begun to set (about 3 minutes). The peel can be slid under the pizza to move it or remove it.

Once you become experienced at handling the pizza and the peel, you may want to take advantage of more of the surface of the pizza stone to cook more than one pizza at a time.

Chicken, Meat and Seafood Pizzas

The Original BBQ Chicken Pizza

The introduction of this pizza at the opening of our Beverly Hills restaurant in 1985 ignited the California Pizza Kitchen craze. We combined great-tasting barbecued chicken with cheese and pizza crust—two all-American favorites in every bite! Instantly popular, it opened our eyes to the infinite potential of non-traditional toppings. Though we have seen it copied throughout the U.S., nobody does it better than the original.

BBQ Chicken Pieces

10 ounces boneless/skinless
    chicken breasts, cut into
    $^3/_4$-inch cubes
1 tablespoon olive oil
2 tablespoons favorite BBQ sauce
    (we use a spicy-sweet sauce)

For the Pizza

1 recipe Basic Pizza Dough
    (page 7)
Cornmeal, semolina or flour
    for handling
$^1/_2$ cup favorite BBQ sauce
    (we use a spicy-sweet sauce)
2 tablespoons shredded smoked
    Gouda cheese
2 cups shredded mozzarella cheese
$^1/_4$ small red onion, sliced into
    $^1/_8$-inch pieces
2 tablespoons chopped
    fresh cilantro

To make BBQ Chicken:

1 In a large frying pan, cook the chicken in olive oil over medium-high heat until just cooked, 5 to 6 minutes. Do not overcook. Set aside in the refrigerator until chilled through. Once chilled, coat the chicken with 2 table-spoons BBQ sauce; set aside in the refrigerator.

To make the pizza:

2 Place the pizza stone in the center of the oven and preheat to 500°F for one hour before cooking pizzas.

See page 9 for directions on handling and shaping the doughs.

3 Use a large spoon to spread $^1/_4$ cup BBQ sauce evenly over the surface of the prepared dough within the rim. Sprinkle 1 tablespoon smoked Gouda cheese over the sauce. Cover with $^3/_4$ cup shredded mozzarella.

4 Distribute half the chicken pieces evenly over the cheese (approximately 18 pieces). Place approximately 18 to 20 pieces of red onion over the surface. Sprinkle an additional $^1/_4$ cup moz-zarella over the top of the pizza.

5 Transfer the pizza to the oven; bake until the crust is crisp and golden and the cheese at the center is bubbly, 8 to 10 minutes. When the pizza is cooked, carefully remove it from the oven; sprinkle 1 tablespoon cilantro over the hot surface. Slice and serve.

6 Repeat with remaining ingredients for a second pizza. (The 2 pizzas may be prepared simultaneously if you are careful in placing the pizzas at opposite corners of your pizza stone.)

Chicken Dijon Pizza

Our newest addition, this pizza was developed out of our love for chicken and mustard and the desire to bring the French culture onto our menu. In truth, we used these very simple ingredients when making sandwiches. So why not pizza? Thus far, the reaction has been très fantastique!

Grilled Garlic Chicken

2 teaspoons minced garlic
1 teaspoon soy sauce
$^1/_2$ teaspoon kosher salt
2 tablespoons olive oil
2 five-ounce boneless/skinless
    chicken breasts

Spinach

1 bunch spinach (frozen
    spinach may be substituted)

Braised Shallots (optional)

1 tablespoon olive oil
6 ounces shallots, peeled and
    separated into 1-inch cloves
$^1/_2$ teaspoon chopped fresh
    thyme (or $^1/_4$ teaspoon
    dried)
1 tablespoon water
$^1/_4$ teaspoon kosher salt
$^1/_4$ teaspoon freshly ground
    black pepper

For the Pizza

1 recipe Basic Pizza Dough
    (page 7)
Cornmeal, semolina or flour for
    handling
2 tablespoons Dijon mustard
1 recipe Caramelized Onions
    (page 25)
$1^1/_2$ cups shredded mozzarella
    cheese

To make Grilled Garlic Chicken:

❶ Prepare a hot grill.

❷ Combine garlic, soy sauce, salt and olive oil. Marinate the chicken breasts in the garlic oil for 10 to 20 minutes.

❸ Grill the chicken breasts for 5 to 7 minutes on each side (discard any uncooked marinade). Remove the cooked chicken from the grill and chill thoroughly. Cut into $^3/_4$-inch cubes; set aside in the refrigerator.

To make the blanched spinach:

❹ Clean and trim spinach leaves. Plunge the leaves into rapidly boiling water for 30 seconds. Transfer the spinach to ice water and stir gently until the spinach is thoroughly chilled. The spinach should be limp and deep, dark green.

5 Drain the spinach and wring out all excess water. Set aside in the refrigerator to continue draining until time to assemble pizza.

To make Braised Shallots:

6 Cook shallots, stirring occasionally, in olive oil over medium heat until lightly browned on all sides, about 3 to 4 minutes. Reduce heat to low, add remaining ingredients and cover. Cook over low heat, covered for approximately ½ hour, stirring or tossing every 4 to 5 minutes. Drain; set aside. The shallots should be soft, translucent and light yellow-brown throughout.

To make the pizza:

7 Place the pizza stone in the center of the oven and preheat to 500°F for one hour before cooking the pizzas.

See page 9 for directions for handling and shaping the doughs.

8 Use a large spoon to spread 1 tablespoon mustard over the surface of the pizza dough, within the rim. Place blanched spinach leaves over the mustard, forming a complete single layer.

9 Spread ¼ cup Caramelized Onions over the spinach and cover the onions with half the mozzarella. Evenly distribute half the Grilled Garlic Chicken over the cheese. Place small cloves of shallot between the chicken pieces.

10 Transfer the pizza to the oven; bake until the crust is crisp and golden and the cheese at the center is bubbly, 8 to 10 minutes.

11 Repeat with remaining ingredients for a second pizza. (The 2 pizzas may be prepared simultaneously if you are careful in placing the pizzas at opposite corners of your pizza stone.)

Rosemary Chicken and Potato Pizza

While plotting expansion into Chicago, we sat in a restaurant and dined on one of the most popular and totally delicious dishes to come out of the Windy City—Chicken Vesuvio. It's chicken roasted in white wine, garlic, lemon, rosemary, oregano, and roasted potato. We said, "If we can do this on a pizza, it would be fantastic." Sure enough, it turned out to be a terrific pizza, one that lets Rick think of his hometown favorite with each bite.

Garlic-Shallot Butter with Lemon

5 tablespoons unsalted butter
$1/4$ cup minced shallot
2 tablespoons minced garlic
1 teaspoon chopped
    fresh thyme leaves
    (or $1/2$ teaspoon dried)
$1/4$ teaspoon salt
Pinch ground white pepper
$1/3$ cup full-bodied chardonnay
1 tablespoon freshly squeezed
    lemon juice
1 teaspoon chicken base or
    bouillon cube (no MSG)

Rosemary Potatoes

$1/2$ pound small red "new"
    potatoes, sliced into $1/8$-inch-
    thick rounds
1 tablespoon minced fresh garlic
1 teaspoon chopped
    fresh oregano leaves
    (or $1/2$ teaspoon dried)
2 teaspoons chopped
    fresh rosemary leaves
    (or 1 teaspoon dried)
$1/4$ teaspoon ground
    white pepper
1 teaspoon kosher salt
2 tablespoons olive oil

Grilled Garlic Chicken

2 teaspoons minced fresh garlic
1 teaspoon soy sauce
$1/2$ teaspoon kosher salt
2 tablespoons olive oil
2 five-ounce boneless/skinless
    chicken breasts

For the Pizza

1 recipe Basic Pizza Dough
    (page 7)
Cornmeal, semolina or
    flour for handling
$1 1/2$ cups shredded
    mozzarella cheese
2 teaspoons chopped
    fresh rosemary leaves
    (or 1 teaspoon dried)
3 teaspoons chopped
    fresh oregano leaves
    (or $1 1/2$ teaspoons dried)
4 teaspoons chopped
    fresh parsley

To make Garlic-Shallot Butter with Lemon:

1 Melt 1 tablespoon butter in a nonstick saucepan over medium-high heat. Add shallot, garlic and thyme. Cook, stirring until mixture is light brown, 7 to 8 minutes.

2 Add salt, pepper, wine, lemon juice and chicken base. Cook until the mixture is reduced to about ½ cup (toward the end of the reduction, reduce the heat to low and stir frequently to prevent scorching).

3 Remove the pan from the heat; quickly and thoroughly whisk in the remaining 4 tablespoons of butter.

To make Rosemary Potatoes:

4 Preheat oven to 325°F. Combine sliced potatoes with the remainder of the ingredients; coat thoroughly. Transfer the potato slices to a sheet pan; spread them out in a single layer, do not overlap. Discard leftover marinade—do not pour it over the potatoes.

5 Cook the potatoes in the preheated oven for approximately 45 minutes. Some of the slices may need to be flipped over to promote even browning. Remove the potatoes from the oven when they

begin to brown. Use a steel spatula to remove the potatoes from the sheet pan. Place potatoes on paper towels at room temperature to drain off any excess oil. Do not refrigerate.

To make Grilled Garlic Chicken:

6 Prepare a hot grill.

7 Combine garlic, soy sauce, salt and olive oil. Marinate the chicken breasts in the garlic oil for about 15 minutes.

8 Grill the chicken breasts for 5 to 7 minutes on each side (discard any uncooked marinade). Remove the cooked chicken from the grill and chill thoroughly. Cut into ½x¾-inch cubes and set aside in the refrigerator.

To make the pizza:

9 Place the pizza stone in the center of the oven and preheat to 500°F for one hour before cooking the pizza.

See page 9 for directions for preparing and shaping the doughs.

10 Use a large spoon to spread 2 tablespoons of Garlic-Shallot Butter over the surface of the prepared pizza dough, within the rim. Cover the butter with half

the mozzarella. Distribute half the grilled garlic chicken evenly over the cheese.

11 Sprinkle half the rosemary and oregano over the chicken. Place the rosemary potatoes over the other toppings, spaced about 1 inch apart.

12 Transfer the pizza to the oven; bake until the crust is crisp and golden and the cheese at the center is bubbly, 8 to 10 minutes. When cooked, carefully remove the pizza from the oven. Sprinkle half the parsley over the hot potato topping. Slice and serve.

13 Repeat with remaining ingredients for a second pizza. (The 2 pizzas may be prepared simultaneously if you are careful in placing the pizzas at opposite corners of your pizza stone.)

Chicken Tostada Pizza

Makes 2 9-inch pizzas

After the success of our BLT pizza, we learned not to be timid about putting salad on a warm pizza crust. And in fact this delicious pizza also led us to create our Caesar Salad Pizza.

Southwestern Black Beans (vegetarian)

$1/2$ pound dried black beans, rinsed and sorted for removal of stones
2 bay leaves
4 cups cold water
1 tablespoon olive oil
1 tablespoon minced fresh garlic
$1/2$ cup finely chopped onion
$1/3$ cup finely chopped bell pepper

1 $14^1/_2$-ounce can ready-cut tomatoes (or use whole canned tomatoes and chop coarsely)
1 teaspoon dried oregano
$1/2$ teaspoon dried thyme
$1/4$ teaspoon cumin
4 cups water
$1/4$ teaspoon chili powder
$1/2$ teaspoon salt

Fried Tortilla Strips
2 cups corn tortillas cut into $1/4$-inch strips
Vegetable oil for frying

For the Pizza

1 recipe Basic Pizza Dough
  (page 7)
Cornmeal, semolina or
  flour for handling
$2/3$ cup shredded Monterey Jack
  cheese
1 recipe Grilled Lime Chicken
  (page 25)
1 cup shredded sharp cheddar
  cheese
4 to 5 cups shredded
  romaine and iceberg lettuces
  ($1/4$-inch strips)
1 cup diced tomatoes
3 ounces creamy ranch
  dressing (use your favorite)
2 tablespoons chopped
  scallions
$1/2$ cup salsa (use your favorite
  or see page 25 for Salsa
  recipe)

To make Southwestern Black Beans:

❶ Boil beans and bay leaves in 4 cups of cold water for 2 minutes; remove from heat and allow the beans to soak in the water for 1 to 2 hours. Or soak the rinsed, sorted beans overnight in room temperature water. Drain beans and discard soaking water.

❷ Cook garlic, onion and bell pepper, stirring occasionally, in olive oil over medium-high heat until onions become translucent, 3 to 4 minutes. Add remainder of bean ingredients including the additional 4 cups of water and reduce heat to low; simmer, stirring occasionally, until all liquid is absorbed into beans, 2 to 3 hours. Set aside in the refrigerator.

To make Fried Tortilla Strips:

❸ Heat oil to deep fry temperature (375°F, just short of smoking). Carefully add strips, turning as necessary to produce an even yellow color. Finished strips should be crispy and golden yellow, not brown. Drain on paper towels. Set aside, uncovered, at room temperature.

To make the pizza:

❹ Place the pizza stone in the center of the oven and preheat to 500°F for one hour before cooking the pizzas.

See page 9 for directions for handling and shaping the doughs.

❺ Use a large spoon to spread $1/3$ cup black beans over the surface of the prepared pizza dough, within the rim. Sprinkle half the Monterey Jack cheese over the beans. Distribute half the grilled chicken pieces over the Monterey Jack cheese; then cover them with half the cheddar cheese.

❻ Transfer the pizza to the oven; bake until the crust is crisp and golden and the cheese at the center is bubbly, 8 to 10 minutes.

❼ Slice the pizza and then top with 2 to $2^{1}/2$ cups shredded lettuce, $1/2$ cup diced tomatoes and half the tortilla strips. Drizzle a generous amount of ranch dressing over the toppings and garnish with 1 tablespoon of chopped scallions. Serve, accompanied by salsa.

❽ Repeat with remaining ingredients for a second pizza. (The 2 pizzas may be prepared simultaneously if you are careful in placing the pizzas at opposite corners of your pizza stone.)

Southwestern Burrito Pizza

MAKES 2 9-INCH PIZZAS

See page 9 for directions for handling and shaping the doughs.

When you think about it—which we happened to do one day—a burrito is not much different than a pizza with the edges folded over.

1 recipe **Basic Pizza Dough** (page 7)

Cornmeal, semolina or flour for handling

1 recipe **Southwestern Black Beans** (page 21)

1 cup **shredded mozzarella cheese**

1 recipe **Grilled Lime Chicken** (page 25)

$^1/_2$ cup **canned Ortega brand chilies, cut into** $^1/_4$**-inch strips, well drained**

20 to 25 **half-rings sweet white onion**

$1^1/_3$ cups **shredded cheddar cheese**

$^1/_2$ cup **sour cream (optional garnish)**

$^1/_4$ cup **green taco sauce (optional garnish)**

To make the pizza:

1 Place the pizza stone in the center of the oven and preheat to 500° F for one hour before cooking pizzas.

See page 9 for directions for handling and shaping the doughs.

2 Use a large spoon to spread $^1/_3$ cup black beans over the surface of the prepared pizza dough, within the rim. Cover the beans with half the shredded mozzarella cheese followed by half the grilled chicken pieces.

3 Distribute half the chili strips and half the onions over the chicken. Cover the toppings with $^2/_3$ cup cheddar cheese.

4 Transfer the pizza to the oven; bake until the crust is crisp and golden and the cheese at the center is bubbly, 9 to 10 minutes.

5 Slice and serve with sour cream and green taco sauce on the side.

6 Repeat with remaining ingredients for a second pizza. (The 2 pizzas may be prepared simultaneously if you are careful in placing the pizzas at opposite corners of your pizza stone.)

Santa Fe Chicken Pizza

Another one of our pioneering pizzas, this pizza resulted from Rick's love of Southwestern food, and our desire to translate this into a pizza. Originally, it was called Grilled Lime Chicken Pizza, after the grilled lime marinated chicken. It acquired the nickname "grilled lime pizza," which just didn't describe this great pizza in a sufficiently appetizing manner. As soon as we changed its name to Santa Fe Chicken it became wildly popular.

Salsa
2 to 3 firm, red, ripe roma (plum) tomatoes ($^1/_2$-inch dice)
2 teaspoons fresh lime juice
1 teaspoon finely minced garlic
$^1/_2$ teaspoon minced jalapeño
1 tablespoon chopped fresh cilantro
Salt to taste

Grilled Lime Chicken
2 five-ounce boneless/skinless chicken breasts
1 tablespoon fresh lime juice
$^1/_2$ teaspoon Worcestershire sauce
$1^1/_2$ teaspoons soy sauce
$^1/_2$ teaspoon honey
Pinch cumin
Pinch dried red pepper flakes
1 tablespoon chopped fresh cilantro
2 tablespoons olive oil

Caramelized Onions
$1^1/_2$ tablespoons unsalted butter
1 small red onion, peeled and sliced into $^1/_8$-inch thick rings
$^1/_4$ teaspoon red wine vinegar
1 teaspoon soy sauce

Guacamole
1 large, ripe, unblemished Haas avocado
1 teaspoon fresh lime juice
1 tablespoon chopped scallions
$^1/_2$ teaspoon finely minced jalapeño pepper
Salt to taste

For the Pizza
1 recipe Basic Pizza Dough (page 7)
Cornmeal, semolina or flour for handling
2 cups shredded mozzarella
2 tablespoons chopped fresh cilantro
$^1/_2$ cup sour cream

To make Salsa:

1 Combine salsa ingredients and set aside in the refrigerator for ½ hour. Place the salsa in a strainer to remove excess water. Set aside in the refrigerator.

To make Grilled Lime Chicken:

2 Prepare a hot grill. Mix the marinade ingredients together. Marinate the breasts for 15 minutes.

3 Grill the breasts for 5 to 7 minutes per side (discard any leftover marinade). Remove the grilled chicken from the grill; chill thoroughly. Cut the cold grilled chicken into ½-inch cubes and set aside in the refrigerator.

To make Caramelized Onions:

4 Melt butter in a small nonstick skillet over medium-high heat and cook the onions, stirring, until they just begin to brown, 3 to 4 minutes. Add vinegar; reduce heat to medium-low and continue cooking for 10 minutes, stirring to prevent scorching.

5 Add soy sauce and cook 5 to 10 minutes longer, stirring. When done, the onions should be quite limp and caramelized brown.

To make Guacamole:

6 Cut the avocado in half; discard pit and scoop the meat away from the skin—discard skin. Using a fork, mash the avocado in a clean bowl; quickly combine with remaining guacamole ingredients.

7 Place clear food wrap directly on the surface of the guacamole and squeeze out air bubbles. Refrigerate until ready for use.

To make the pizza:

8 Place the pizza stone in the center of the oven and preheat to 500°F for one hour before cooking the pizzas.

See page 9 for directions for handling and shaping the doughs.

9 Distribute half the sautéed onions over the surface of the stretched dough. Cover the onions with ¾ cup mozzarella.

10 Evenly distribute half the grilled lime chicken over the cheese. Sprinkle an additional ¼ cup mozzarella over the chicken.

11 Transfer the pizza to the oven; bake until the crust is crisp and golden and the cheese at the center is bubbly, 8 to 10 minutes.

12 When the pizza is cooked, carefully remove it from the oven. Sprinkle 1 tablespoon cilantro over the hot cheese and slice the pizza. Serve with salsa, sour cream and guacamole.

13 Repeat with remaining ingredients for a second pizza. (The 2 pizzas may be prepared simultaneously if you are careful in placing the pizzas at opposite corners of your pizza stone.)

Tandoori Chicken Pizza

This pizza illustrates how many different types of world cuisine can be represented on a pizza, and why you should let your imagination fly. We fell in love with the Chicken Tika served at a small Indian restaurant and then captured the same exotic quality, dramatic red color and taste on a pizza. It's doubtful you'll find this in a pizza parlor in India, but you can indeed put Indian food on a pizza.

Tomato-Yogurt Curry

1 teaspoon olive oil
1 teaspoon minced fresh garlic
$1/2$ cup diced or chopped (canned) tomatoes
1 teaspoon chopped fresh ginger
$1/8$ teaspoon cumin
1 teaspoon garam masala (a spice available at Indian markets)
$1/4$ teaspoon minced fresh jalapeño pepper
$1/4$ cup chicken stock (preferably homemade)
$1/4$ cup low-fat plain yogurt
1 teaspoon chopped fresh cilantro
1 tablespoon unsalted butter

Tandoori Chicken

1 teaspoon chopped fresh ginger
1 teaspoon minced fresh garlic
$1/2$ teaspoon minced fresh jalapeño pepper
2 tablespoon tandoori paste (available at gourmet specialty stores and Indian markets)
2 tablespoons low-fat plain yogurt
1 tablespoon unsalted butter, melted
2 five-ounce boneless/skinless chicken breasts

For the Pizza

1 recipe Honey-Wheat Pizza Dough (page 7)
Cornmeal, semolina or flour for handling
$1/2$ small zucchini
$1/2$ small yellow crookneck squash, sliced into $1/8$-inch-thick pieces
$1^{1}/_{2}$ cups shredded mozzarella cheese
2 tablespoons chopped fresh cilantro
$1/2$ cup Major Grey's mango chutney (available in gourmet markets)

21

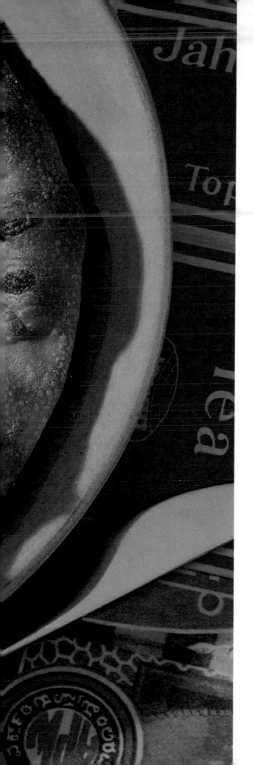

To make Tomato-Yogurt Curry:

1 Heat garlic in olive oil over medium heat until it becomes translucent, 1 to 2 minutes. Add next 7 ingredients (through yogurt); reduce heat and boil the mixture until all excess liquid has evaporated, approximately 3 minutes. Turn off burner and quickly blend in cilantro and butter; set aside.

To make Tandoori Chicken:

2 Combine first 5 ingredients (through yogurt). Coat the chicken breast with the resulting mixture. (Plastic gloves will prevent your fingers from turning red.) Pour the butter over the marinating chicken breasts and stir to coat well.

3 Prepare a hot grill. Grill the chicken for 5 to 7 minutes per side (discard marinade—do not reuse). Remove from the grill and chill thoroughly. Slice the chilled chicken into $\frac{1}{8}$-inch thick slices and set aside in the refrigerator.

To make the pizza:

4 Place the pizza stone in the center of the oven and preheat to 500°F for one hour before cooking the pizzas.

See page 9 for directions for preparing and shaping the doughs.

5 Use a large spoon to spread $\frac{1}{4}$ cup Tomato-Yogurt Curry evenly over the surface of the prepared pizza dough within the rim. Place slices of yellow and green squashes over the sauce—do not overlap.

6 Cover the sauced area with half the mozzarella and distribute half the sliced Tandoori Chicken evenly over the cheese.

7 Transfer the pizza to the oven, bake until the crust is crisp and golden and the cheese at the center is bubbly, 8 to 10 minutes. Carefully remove the pizza from the oven and sprinkle 1 tablespoon chopped fresh cilantro over the top. Slice and serve, accompanied by mango chutney.

8 Repeat with remaining ingredients for a second pizza. (The 2 pizzas may be prepared simultaneously if you are careful in placing the pizzas at opposite corners of your pizza stone.)

Thai Chicken Pizza

This is a very nostalgic pizza to us, because it's one of the first we sank our creative teeth into. Back when we were still attorneys, Larry made a spicy chicken pasta salad with a delicious, Thai-inspired spicy peanut, ginger and sesame satay. When we began making pizzas, we thought it would make a pretty good one if we could successfully transfer it, particularly since chicken was such a hot item. We were right. After we finished it off with carrots, cilantro and bean sprouts, it quickly became one of our most popular pizzas.

Spicy Peanut Sauce

$1/2$ cup peanut butter
$1/2$ cup hoisin sauce
1 tablespoon honey
2 teaspoons red wine vinegar
2 teaspoons minced ginger
2 tablespoons roasted sesame oil
2 teaspoons soy sauce
1 teaspoon Vietnamese chili
    sauce (or dried chili flakes)
1 tablespoon oyster sauce
2 tablespoons water

Thai Chicken Pieces

1 tablespoon olive oil
10 ounces boneless/skinless
    chicken breast, cut into
    $3/4$-inch cubes

For the Pizza

1 recipe Basic Pizza Dough
    (page 7)
Cornmeal, semolina or
    flour for handling
2 cups shredded
    mozzarella cheese
4 scallions, slivered diagonally
    oriental style

$1/2$ cup white bean sprouts
$1/4$ cup shredded carrot
2 tablespoons chopped,
    roasted peanuts
2 tablespoons chopped
    fresh cilantro

To make Spicy Peanut Sauce:

❶ Combine sauce ingredients in a small pan over medium heat. Bring the sauce to a boil; boil gently for one minute. Divide into two portions for use on chicken and pizza; set aside.

To make Thai Chicken:

❷ Cook the chicken in olive oil over medium-high heat, stirring, until just cooked, 5 to 6 minutes. Do not overcook. Set aside in the refrigerator until chilled through. Once chilled, coat the chicken with $1/4$ cup Spicy Peanut Sauce. Set aside in the refrigerator.

To make the pizza:

3 Place the pizza stone in the center of the oven and preheat to 500°F for one hour before cooking the pizzas.

See page 9 for directions for handling and shaping the doughs.

4 Use a large spoon to spread ¼ cup spicy peanut sauce evenly over the surface of the prepared dough within the rim. Cover the sauce with ¾ cup shredded mozzarella.

5 Distribute half the chicken pieces evenly over the cheese followed by half the green onions, bean sprouts and carrots, respectively. Sprinkle an additional ¼ cup shredded mozzarella over the other toppings and top the pizza with 1 tablespoon chopped roasted peanuts.

6 Transfer the pizza to the oven; bake until the crust is crisp and golden and the cheese at the center is bubbly, 9 to 10 minutes. When cooked through, carefully remove the pizza from the oven. Sprinkle 1 tablespoon chopped fresh cilantro over the hot, cheesy surface. Slice and serve.

7 Repeat with remaining ingredients for a second pizza. (The 2 pizzas may be prepared simultaneously if you are careful in placing the pizzas at opposite corners of your pizza stone.)

Chicken Teriyaki Pizza

We created this pizza at home while being interviewed for L.A. Magazine. The reporter asked if we could create a new pizza on the spur of the moment. That afternoon we experimented with various sauces—sweet, sour, soy, garlic—and eventually decided on the sweeter one, which we personally liked. You may substitute any teriyaki sauce that suits your preference.

CPK Teriyaki Sauce

$^1/_2$ cup Kikkoman® teriyaki sauce
$^1/_4$ cup orange marmalade
1 teaspoon minced fresh garlic
$1^1/_2$ teaspoons minced fresh ginger
2 tablespoons dark brown sugar
3 tablespoons all-purpose flour
3 tablespoons water

Teriyaki Chicken

2 five-ounce boneless/skinless chicken breasts
2 tablespoons Kikkoman® teriyaki sauce
$^1/_2$ teaspoon minced fresh garlic
$^1/_2$ teaspoon minced fresh ginger
2 teaspoons olive oil

For the Pizza

1 recipe Basic Pizza Dough (page 7)
Cornmeal, semolina or flour for handling
$1^1/_3$ cup shredded mozzarella cheese
40 to 50 red onion half-rings, $^1/_8$ inch thick
6 small scallions, white parts sliced oriental style; green ends chopped into $^1/_4$-inch pieces

18 to 20 strips red bell pepper ($^1/_8$x $2^1/_2$ inches)
18 to 20 strips yellow bell pepper ($^1/_8$x $2^1/_2$ inches)

To make CPK Teriyaki Sauce:

❶ Mix flour and water together (no lumps) in a small mixing bowl; set aside.

❷ Combine all other sauce ingredients in a small saucepan over medium heat. Bring to a boil and cook for 1 minute, stirring frequently; remove from heat. Pour $^1/_4$ cup of the boiled mixture into the flour/water paste while stirring vigorously to keep lumps from forming.

❸ Whisk the flour mixture back into the remainder of the sauce; mix thoroughly. Return to heat and boil, stirring constantly, for $^1/_2$ minute; set aside.

To make Teriyaki Chicken:

4 Prepare a hot grill.

5 Combine all chicken ingredients and allow chicken to marinate for 10 minutes. Grill the breasts for 5 to 6 minutes per side. When done, remove from grill and chill thoroughly.

6 Slice the chilled breasts into ¼-inch thick strips. Set aside in the refrigerator.

To make the pizza:

7 Place the pizza stone in the center of the oven and preheat to 500°F for one hour before cooking the pizzas.

See page 9 for directions for handling and shaping the doughs.

8 Use a large spoon to spread 3 tablespoons of CPK Teriyaki Sauce over the surface of the prepared pizza dough, within the rim. Cover the sauce with ⅔ cup mozzarella. Distribute 20 to 24 red onion half-rings, half the slivered scallions and half the pepper strips over the cheese. Distribute half the teriyaki chicken strips over the vegetables.

9 Transfer the pizza to the oven; bake until the crust is crisp and golden and the cheese at the center is bubbly, 8 to 10 minutes.

10 When the pizza is done, carefully remove it from the oven. Slice and garnish with chopped scallions (the dark green part). Serve immediately.

11 Repeat with the remaining ingredients for a second pizza. (The 2 pizzas may be prepared simultaneously if you are careful in placing the pizzas at opposite sides of your pizza stone).

33

will feast on a culinary delight.

Moo Shu Chicken Calzone

As the old Chinese proverb says, "Once it occurs to you that you can wrap your moo shu in a calzone rather than the traditional rice pancake, do it."

Moo Shu Chicken

10 ounces boneless/skinless chicken (preferably thigh meat)
1 bay leaf
1 sprig fresh thyme
4 whole black peppercorns
1 quart cold water
2 tablespoons hoisin sauce

Sautéed Mushrooms

1 cup white mushrooms, sliced $1/8$ inch thick
$1/2$ cup oyster mushroom tops, sliced into $1/2$-inch strips
$1/2$ cup shiitake mushroom tops, sliced into $1/2$-inch strips
1 tablespoon olive oil
$1/4$ teaspoon kosher salt
$1/8$ teaspoon ground black pepper

For the Calzone

1 recipe Basic Pizza Dough (page 7)
Cornmeal, semolina or flour for handling
1 whole egg, mixed with 1 teaspoon cold water (for sealing calzones)
$1/2$ cup hoisin sauce
1 teaspoon minced fresh ginger
$1^1/2$ cups shredded mozzarella cheese
$1/2$ cup white bean sprouts
6 scallions, white part only, slivered oriental style
3 tablespoons roasted sesame oil

35

To make Moo Shu Chicken:

1 Place all ingredients except hoisin sauce in a saucepan over high heat. When the water boils, reduce heat to a low boil and cook the chicken for 10 minutes.

2 Remove chicken; drain well. Discard water. Chill chicken thoroughly. Cut the chilled chicken into ¼-inch strips. Coat with hoisin sauce. Set aside in the refrigerator.

To make Sautéed Mushrooms:

3 Heat oil in a nonstick sauté pan until it begins to smoke. Add mushrooms, tossing immediately and frequently. Add salt and pepper; cook mushrooms for about 5 minutes or until all juices evaporate and mushrooms are fully cooked. Set aside in the refrigerator.

To make the calzone:

4 Place the pizza stone in the center of the oven and preheat to 500°F for one hour before cooking the calzones.

See page 9 for directions for handling and shaping the doughs. However, when making calzones it is not necessary or desirable to form a lip. Instead, use a rolling pin or your hands to form a 9 to 10-inch flat circle. Place the dough on a square of aluminum foil.

5 Brush the egg-and-water mixture in a 1-inch stripe along the edge of one half of the dough. (This will act as the "glue" to seal the calzone closed.)

6 Mix the ginger into the hoisin sauce and spread 2 tablespoons of this sauce over the center of the dough. Keep this and all other ingredients 1½ inches away from the edges. Spread ¾ cup mozzarella over the sauce.

7 Cover the cheese with half the chicken pieces, green onions, sautéed mushrooms and bean sprouts (crush the bean sprouts slightly to keep them from poking holes in the dough when you fold it over).

8 Pull the non-egg-coated side of the dough over the top of the filling, pressing the edges of the dough together with fingers or a spoon to form a complete seal. If desired, you can use a pizza wheel to trim off excess uneven edges.

9 Brush the top of the calzone with sesame oil and transfer the calzone on its foil onto the pizza stone in the oven. Cook for approximately 10 minutes, until the calzone is lightly browned and puffed all over. If necessary, you can turn the calzone using the corner of the foil to promote even browning.

10 When the calzone is done, carefully remove it from the oven and transfer to a serving plate. Brush additional sesame oil over the still-hot crust. Be extremely careful when slicing to avoid burns from escaping steam. Extra hoisin and scallions may be used as accompaniments.

11 Repeat with remaining ingredients for a second calzone. (The 2 calzones may be prepared simultaneously if you are careful in placing the calzones at opposite corners of your pizza stone.)

Peking Duck Pizza

Peking Duck

1 pound boneless duck breast,
  skin on
2 tablespoons hoisin sauce

Fried Won Tons

10 small won ton wrappers,
  cut into $1/2$-inch strips
1 cup olive oil for deep frying

For the Pizza

1 recipe Basic Pizza Dough
  (page 7)
Cornmeal, semolina or
  flour for handling
$1/4$ cup hoisin sauce, in a
  ketchup-type squeeze bottle.
$1^{1}/2$ cups shredded mozzarella
  cheese
8 scallions, white part only,
  slivered oriental style
1 recipe Sautéed Mushrooms
  (page 35)

More than others, this pizza taught us to be mindful of what the oven would do to the various ingredients in arriving at a final taste of perfection. Did we need to precook some ingredients and not others? The original version had the duck cooked on top of the pizza. However, after much trial and error, we now roast the duck breast in hoisin sauce and then set it on the pizza, and it's a wonderful mix of taste and cultures. Larry has always contended that America's love of hoisin sauce has driven the popularity of this pizza.

To make Peking Duck:

1 Preheat oven to 350°F.

2 Coat duck breast with hoisin sauce on all surfaces, including under the skin. Roast the breast skin side up for $1^{1}/2$ hours. When cooked, discard fat and chill the breast thoroughly. When chilled, discard skin and slice the breast into $1/8$-inch-thick slices. Set aside in the refrigerator.

To make Fried Won Tons:

3 Heat oil to 375°F (just short of smoking temperature).

4 Fry won ton strips in batches for 30 to 45 seconds. They should become rosy/golden brown, blistered and crisp. Drain on paper towels. Set aside, uncovered, at room temperature.

To make the pizza:

5 Place the pizza stone in the center of the oven and preheat to 500°F for one hour before cooking the pizzas.

See page 9 for directions for handling and shaping the doughs.

6 Squeeze a small amount (1 to 2 teaspoons) of hoisin sauce over the surface of the prepared pizza dough, within the rim. Cover the sauced area with half the mozzarella. Distribute about 2 tablespoons of slivered green onions over the cheese. Place slices of Peking Duck, evenly spaced, over the cheese and onions. Spread half the sautéed mushrooms over the duck.

7 Transfer the pizza to the oven; bake until the crust is crisp and golden and the cheese at the center is bubbly, 9 to 10 minutes.

8 Slice the pizza, and then top with half the fried won tons. Squeeze about 1 tablespoon hoisin sauce over the won tons in a "spiderweb" pattern. Garnish with more slivered green onions; serve immediately.

9 Repeat with remaining ingredients for a second pizza. (The 2 pizzas may be prepared simultaneously if you are careful in placing the pizzas at opposite corners of your pizza stone.)

Peking Duck Pizza

BLT Pizza

If inspiration can be traced to its origin, this pizza is the direct result of Larry's craving for mayonnaise. What can't be told through pictures and stories is recreated in food, and those who order this pizza love it. In fact, we once served a variety of our pizzas to the audience of a national TV show and they named our BLT as their favorite. When the warm, savory pizza is topped with the refreshing lettuce and mayo, it's unbeatable.

1 recipe Basic Pizza Dough (page 7)
Cornmeal, semolina or flour for handling
2 tablespoons extra virgin olive oil
2 cups shredded mozzarella cheese
$^1/_2$ cup crumbled, crisp cooked bacon
1 to 2 roma (plum) tomatoes, sliced into $^1/_8$-inch-thick rounds
3 cups chopped romaine lettuce
4 tablespoons mayonnaise

To make the pizza:

❶ Place the pizza stone in the center of the oven and preheat to 500°F for one hour before cooking the pizzas.

See page 9 for directions for handling and shaping the doughs.

❷ Brush 1 tablespoon olive oil over the surface of the prepared dough, within the rim. Spread $^3/_4$ cup mozzarella over the oiled surface. Distribute $^1/_4$ cup bacon over the cheese.

❸ Place 8 to 9 tomato slices over the bacon, spaced about 1 inch apart. Sprinkle an additional $^1/_4$ cup mozzarella over the tomatoes.

❹ Transfer the pizza to the oven; bake until the crust is crisp and golden and the cheese at the center is bubbly, 8 to 10 minutes.

❺ Carefully remove the pizza from the oven and slice into 6 pieces. Mix 2 tablespoons mayonnaise with $1^1/_2$ cups chopped romaine. Spread the dressed lettuce over the surface of the pizza. Serve immediately.

❻ Repeat with remaining ingredients for a second pizza. (The 2 pizzas may be prepared simultaneously if you are careful in placing the pizzas at opposite corners of your pizza stone.)

Chicken Caesar Salad Pizza

MAKES 2 9-INCH PIZZAS

CPK Caesar Dressing

1$^1/_2$ teaspoons minced
    fresh garlic
1$^1/_2$ teaspoons minced shallots
1 teaspoon anchovy paste
$^1/_2$ teaspoon chopped fresh
    oregano leaves
1 teaspoon freshly squeezed
    lemon juice
1 tablespoon red wine vinegar
1 teaspoon drained
    nonpareil capers
$^1/_2$ cup extra virgin olive oil

For the Pizza

1 recipe Basic Pizza Dough
    (page 7)
Cornmeal semolina or
    flour for handling
1$^1/_2$ cups shredded
    mozzarella cheese
1 recipe Grilled Garlic Chicken
    (page 16)
4 cups chilled romaine lettuce,
    cut into 1-inch squares
    (other lettuces may be
    added or substituted)
2 tablespoons grated
    parmesan cheese

*For years people who loved
our Caesar Salad asked,
"Why don't you make a
Caesar salad pizza?"
They were right! With the
addition of chicken and
warm cheese topping and
our delicious crust, we've
created a taste sensation
that we believe would
make Caesar proud.*

To make CPK Caesar Dressing:

1 Process all ingredients except oil using a hand-held propeller-type mixer (or use a whisk in a small bowl). Slowly blend in oil; set aside.

To make the pizza:

2 Place the pizza stone in the center of the oven and preheat to 500°F for one hour before cooking pizzas.

See page 9 for directions for handling and shaping the doughs.

3 Brush or spread a thin coating of Caesar dressing over the surface of the prepared dough within the rim. Cover the dressing with half the mozzarella. Distribute half the chicken pieces evenly over the cheese.

4 Transfer the pizza to the oven; bake until the crust is crisp and golden and the cheese at the center is bubbly, 8 to 10 minutes.

5 When the pizza is cooked, carefully remove from the oven. Toss 2 cups of lettuce together with 2 tablespoons Caesar dressing. Slice the pizza and spread the dressed greens over the top of the pizza. Sprinkle 1 tablespoon parmesan cheese over the top and serve immediately.

6 Repeat with remaining ingredients for a second pizza. (The 2 pizzas may be prepared simultaneously if you are careful in placing the pizzas at opposite corners of your pizza stone.)

Hawaiian Pizza

MAKES 2 9-INCH PIZZAS

One day Rick asked his son, Ian, to name his favorite pizza. "Dad," he said, "it's not on the menu." Then he described the pizza that he and his friends ate—Canadian bacon and pineapple. Soon after, it was on the menu. Mahalo.

1 recipe Basic Pizza dough
   (page 7)
Cornmeal, semolina or
   flour for handling
1 recipe Tomato Sauce
   (page 64)
2 cups shredded
   mozzarella cheese
6 thin rounds Canadian-style
   bacon, cut into quarters
24 to 30 one-inch chunks
   fresh pineapple, drained

To make the pizza:

1 Place the pizza stone in the center of the oven and preheat to 500°F for one hour before cooking the pizzas.

See page 9 for directions for handling and shaping the doughs.

2 Use a large spoon to evenly spread ¼ cup Tomato Sauce over the surface of the prepared dough, within the rim. Cover the sauce with ¾ cup mozzarella.

3 Distribute half the Canadian-style bacon over the cheese followed by half the pineapple. Sprinkle an additional ¼ cup mozzarella over the top.

4 Transfer the pizza to the oven; bake until the crust is crisp and golden and the cheese at the center is bubbly, 8 to 10 minutes.

5 Repeat with remaining ingredients for a second pizza. (The 2 pizzas may be prepared simultaneously if you are careful in placing the pizzas at opposite corners of your pizza stone.)

Mushroom, Pepperoni and Sausage Pizza

MAKES 2 9-INCH PIZZAS

It's downright hard to be a pizza restaurant without offering this staple. It would be like an ice cream parlor not serving vanilla, chocolate or strawberry. Traditionalists love our version of this classic, and indeed it's one of our most popular pizzas.

1 recipe Basic Pizza Dough (page 7)
Cornmeal, semolina or flour for handling
1 recipe Tomato Sauce (page 64)
2 cups shredded mozzarella cheese
$^1/_4$ pound mild Italian (fennel) sausage, cooked and drained
$^2/_3$ cup thin sliced white mushrooms
36 slices pepperoni

To make the pizza:

❶ Place the pizza stone in the center of the oven and preheat to 500°F for one hour before cooking the pizzas.

See page 9 for directions for handling and shaping the doughs.

❷ Use a large spoon to spread $^1/_4$ cup Tomato Sauce evenly over the surface of the prepared dough, within the rim. Cover the sauce with $^3/_4$ cup shredded mozzarella.

❸ Crumble $^1/_4$ cup cooked sausage over the cheese followed by half the mushrooms. Place half the slices of pepperoni over the other toppings. Sprinkle an additional $^1/_4$ cup mozzarella over the top.

❹ Transfer the pizza to the oven; bake until the crust is crisp and golden and the cheese at the center is bubbly, 8 to 10 minutes.

❺ Repeat with remaining ingredients for a second pizza. (The 2 pizzas may be prepared simultaneously if you are careful in placing the pizzas at opposite corners of your pizza stone.)

Top *Mushroom, Pepperoni and Sausage Pizza;* **Bottom** *Goat Cheese Pizza (recipe on next page)*

Goat Cheese Pizza

1 tablespoon olive oil
1 recipe Basic Pizza Dough
   (page 7)
Cornmeal, semolina or
   flour for handling
2 cups shredded
   mozzarella cheese
$\frac{1}{2}$ cup crumbled, crisp
   cooked bacon
2 roma (plum) tomatoes sliced
   into $\frac{1}{8}$-inch-thick rounds
12 strips red bell pepper
   (2 x $\frac{1}{8}$ inch)
12 strips yellow bell pepper
   (2 x $\frac{1}{8}$ inch)
12 strips green bell pepper
   (2 x $\frac{1}{8}$ inch)
24 pieces red onion,
   (2 x $\frac{1}{8}$ inch)
2 ounces mild goat cheese,
   such as Chevre or
   Montrachet

To make the pizza:

1 Place the pizza stone in the center of the oven and preheat to 500°F for one hour before cooking pizzas.

See page 9 for directions for handling and shaping the doughs.

One of our brightest, most colorful, eye-catching pizzas, this one was around near the beginning, a reminder of the innocent, early days when California pizza was just created. After several years, we figured people might be tired of something foodwriters made a cliche. But we were wrong. There was such an uproar among its loyal supporters that we had no choice except to put this pizza back on the menu.

2 Brush a light coating of olive oil over the surface of the pizza up to the rim. Spread $\frac{3}{4}$ cup mozzarella over the oiled surface. Sprinkle $\frac{1}{4}$ cup bacon over the cheese.

3 Place half the tomato slices, spaced 1 inch apart over the top of the pizza—don't overlap. Spread half the pepper strips and onion pieces over the tomatoes.

4 Sprinkle additional $\frac{1}{4}$ cup mozzarella over the pizza. Crumble 1 ounce goat cheese over the other toppings (approximately 12 small pinches).

5 Transfer the pizza to the oven; bake until the crust is crisp and golden and the cheese at the center is bubbly, 8 to 10 minutes. When the pizza is fully cooked, carefully remove it from the oven. Slice and serve.

6 Repeat with remaining ingredients for a second pizza. (The 2 pizzas may be prepared simultaneously if you are careful in placing the pizzas at opposite corners of your pizza stone.)

Shrimp Scampi Pizza

*Shakespeare asked,
"What's in a name?"
This pizza taught us the
answer is, "A lot."
Originally, we called this
Roasted Garlic Shrimp
pizza, and people ignored
it. However, we changed its
name on the menu to
Shrimp Scampi, thus
capturing the romance of
a familiar dish.*

Garlic-Shallot Butter

5 tablespoons unsalted butter
$^1/_4$ cup minced shallot
2 tablespoons minced garlic
1 teaspoon chopped
   fresh thyme leaves
   (or $^1/_2$ teaspoon dried)
$^1/_4$ teaspoon salt
Pinch ground white pepper
$^1/_3$ cup full-bodied chardonnay
1 tablespoon freshly squeezed
   lemon juice
1 teaspoon chicken base or
   bouillon cube (no MSG)

Roasted Garlic

$^1/_3$ cup coarsely chopped garlic
$^1/_2$ teaspoon olive oil

For the Pizza

1 recipe Basic Pizza Dough
   (page 7)
Cornmeal, semolina or
   flour for handling
$1^1/_2$ cups shredded
   mozzarella cheese
$^1/_4$ white onion, sliced into
   $^1/_8$-inch-thick half-rings
12 medium shrimp, peeled,
   deveined and cut in half
   lengthwise
4 teaspoons chopped
   fresh oregano leaves
   (or 2 teaspoons dried)
2 tablespoons chopped
   Italian parsley

To make Garlic-Shallot Butter:

❶ Melt 1 tablespoon butter in a nonstick saucepan over medium-high heat. Add shallot, garlic and thyme. Cook, stirring, until mixture is light brown, 7 to 8 minutes.

❷ Add salt, pepper, wine, lemon juice and chicken base. Cook until the mixture is reduced to about ½ cup. (Toward the end of the reduction, reduce the heat to low and stir frequently to prevent scorching.)

❸ Remove the pan from the burner; quickly and thoroughly whisk in the remaining 4 table-spoons butter.

To make Roasted Garlic:

❹ Preheat the oven to 325°F. Coat the coarsely chopped garlic with oil. Spread the pieces of garlic over the surface of a glass casserole or sheet pan. Roast in the preheated oven for 25 to 30 minutes, until the edges of the garlic begin to brown. Remove the garlic from the oven. Scrape up the garlic and redistribute it in a single layer to provide even browning. Return the garlic to the oven for another 15 minutes. Remove the garlic from the oven when it is uniformly golden brown. Set aside for pizza assembly.

To make the pizza:

❺ Place the pizza stone in the center of the oven and preheat for 500°F for one hour before cooking the pizza.

See page 9 for directions for preparing and shaping the doughs.

❻ Use a large spoon to spread 2 tablespoons of the Garlic-Shallot Butter over the surface of the crust, within the rim. Spread ¾ cup mozzarella over the butter sauce.

❼ Evenly distribute half the onions and half the roasted garlic over the cheese. Place 12 shrimp halves, skin side up, evenly over the cheese and toppings.

❽ Transfer the pizza to the oven; bake until the crust is crisp and golden and the cheese at the center is bubbly, 8 to 10 minutes. The shrimp should be opaque and cooked through. When the pizza is fully cooked, carefully remove from the oven. Sprinkle half the oregano and parsley over the cheese. Slice and serve.

❾ Repeat with remaining ingredients for a second pizza. (The 2 pizzas may be prepared simultaneously if you are careful in placing the pizzas at opposite corners of your pizza stone.)

Note: *Grilled Garlic Chicken (page 16) may be substituted for the shrimp.*

Shrimp Scampi Pizza

Shrimp Pesto Pizza

MAKES 2 9-INCH PIZZAS

In terms of flavor, this is one of the most assertive pizzas we have ever devised. Not only is it richly colorful, but the deep green pesto, red sun-dried tomatoes, black Kalamata olives and white and pink shrimp all have distinctive tastes that stand out even more when combined on a single crust.

Pesto

$1/2$ cup fresh basil leaves (firmly packed)
1 teaspoon minced fresh garlic
$1^1/2$ ounces pine nuts
$1/4$ cup grated parmesan cheese
$1/3$ cup extra virgin olive oil

For the Pizza

1 recipe Basic Pizza Dough (page 7)
Cornmeal, semolina or flour for handling
2 cups shredded mozzarella cheese
1 to 2 roma (plum) tomatoes, sliced into $1/8$-inch-thick rounds
6 Kalamata olives, pitted and sliced into sixths
6 oil-packed sun-dried tomatoes, drained and cut into $1/8$-inch strips
12 medium shrimp, peeled, deveined and cut in half lengthwise

To make Pesto:

❶ Combine the basil, olive oil, pine nuts and garlic in the work bowl of your food processor with a steel knife attachment. Process at high speed; stop frequently to scrape down the sides of the bowl until the contents are completely pureed/blended.

❷ Transfer to a small bowl and blend in cheese by hand. When thoroughly blended, cover closely with clear plastic wrap and set aside in the refrigerator. (Allow pesto to come to room temperature before assembling pizza.)

To make the pizza:

❸ Place the pizza stone in the center of the oven and preheat to 500°F for one hour before cooking the pizzas.

See page 9 for directions for handling and shaping the doughs.

❹ Use the back of a spoon to spread 2 tablespoons pesto evenly over the surface of the prepared pizza dough, within the rim. Cover the pesto with $3/4$ cup shredded mozzarella.

❺ Place tomato slices over the cheese, evenly spaced approximately 1 inch apart. Distribute about 18 strips sun-dried tomatoes and 18 olive slices over the tomatoes. Sprinkle an additional $1/4$ cup mozzarella over the other ingredients. Place 12 shrimp halves, skin side up, over the top of the pizza.

6 Transfer the pizza to the oven; bake until the crust is crisp and golden and the cheese at the center is bubbly, 8 to 10 minutes. The shrimp should be opaque and cooked through.

7 Repeat with remaining ingredients for a second pizza. (The 2 pizzas may be prepared simultaneously if you are careful in placing the pizzas at opposite corners of your pizza stone.)

Smoked Salmon Appetizer Pizza

MAKES FOUR 6-INCH PIZZAS OR TWO 9-INCH PIZZAS

Dill-Shallot Sauce

$1/2$ **cup sour cream**

2 **teaspoons minced
fresh shallots**

1 **tablespoon chopped
fresh baby dill leaves**

$1/2$ **teaspoon freshly squeezed
lemon juice**

Small pinch kosher salt

For the Pizza

1 **recipe Basic Pizza Dough
(page 7)**

**Cornmeal, semolina or
flour for handling**

3 **tablespoons olive oil**

1 **cup thinly sliced red onions**

8 **to 10 ounces Norwegian
smoked salmon**

2 **tablespoons capers
(optional garnish)**

4 **dill sprigs (optional garnish)**

*We originally tried this
pizza on our brunch
menu—our interpretation
of a bagel with cream
cheese and lox. It's about
that easy to make, too.*

To make Dill-Shallot Sauce:

❶ Combine all sauce ingredients, mix thoroughly and set aside in the refrigerator.

To make the pizza:

❷ Place the pizza stone in the center of the oven and preheat to 500°F for one hour before cooking the pizzas.

See page 9 for directions for handling and shaping the doughs. Separate the dough into 4 equal pieces for final proofing.

❸ Brush olive oil over the surface of the prepared pizza dough, within the rim. Distribute ¼ cup sliced red onions over the oil.

❹ Transfer the onion-covered dough to the oven; cook until the dough begins to brown, about 5 minutes. Check the oven during cooking and pop any large bubbles that form in the center area of the crust with a fork.

❺ When the crust is done, carefully remove it from the oven. Use a spoon to spread 2 tablespoons Dill-Shallot Sauce over the onion-covered surface (2 tablespoons are required for a 6-inch mini pizza; if making a regular 8- to 9-inch pizza, about ¼ cup is required).

❻ Place slices of smoked salmon over the Dill-Shallot Sauce, forming a single, complete layer. Slice and garnish with capers and dill, if desired. Serve while the crust is still warm.

❼ Repeat with additional ingredients for three more mini pizzas or one more regular-sized pizza. These additional pizzas may be done simultaneously, if so desired.

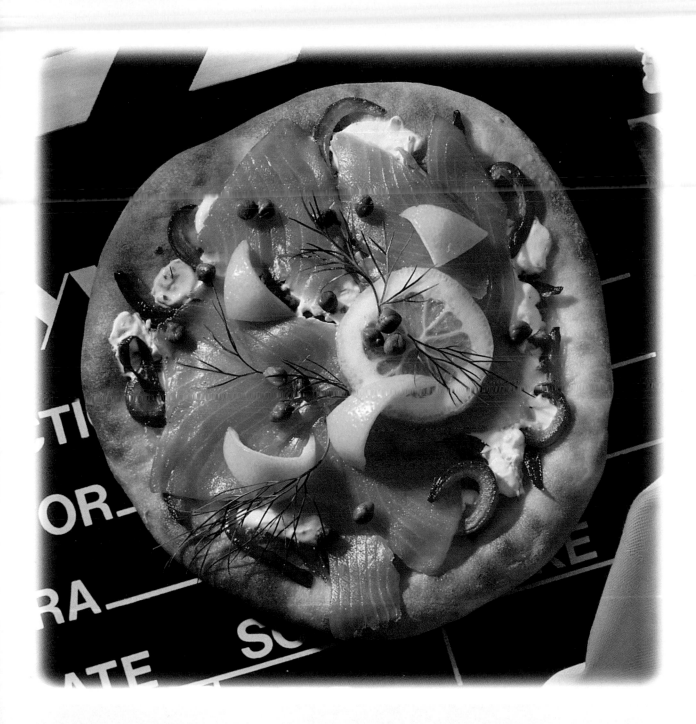

Vegetarian Pizzas

Five-Cheese Pizza

First we did a 3-cheese pizza, but then we entered and won a contest at a Peach Festival in Georgia when we came up with a 5-cheese, basil and sliced peach pizza.

We called it Savannah Pizza. It was surprisingly great, and so we kept serving it substituting ripe tomatoes for the peaches, which means it never goes out of season. (Of course, you could make the original.)

1 recipe Basic Pizza Dough (page 7)

Cornmeal, semolina or flour for handling

2 tablespoons extra virgin olive oil

2 tablespoons shredded smoked Gouda cheese

3/4 cup shredded mozzarella cheese

1/2 cup shredded Swedish Fontina cheese

1 to 2 roma (plum) tomatoes, sliced into 1/8-inch-thick rounds

3 ounces buffalo mozzarella or fresh "water-packed" mozzarella (cut into 24 1-inch pieces)

1/2 cup (2 ounces) shaved romano cheese

2 tablespoons chiffonade of fresh basil

To make the pizza:

❶ Place the pizza stone in the center of the oven and preheat to 500°F for one hour before cooking the pizzas.

See page 9 for directions for handling and shaping the doughs.

❷ Brush the surface of the prepared dough with a thin application of olive oil. Evenly distribute the cheese over the oiled surface as follows: 1 tablespoon smoked Gouda, 1/3 cup mozzarella and 1/4 cup Fontina.

❸ Place tomato slices over the cheeses, spaced about 1 inch apart—do not overlap or "black out" the surface. Top the tomatoes with half the pieces of buffalo mozzarella followed by half the shaved romano.

❹ Transfer the pizza to the oven; bake until the crust is crisp and golden and the cheese at the center is bubbly, 8 to 10 minutes. Remove pizza from oven. Sprinkle 1 tablespoon fresh basil over the hot, cheesy surface. Slice and serve.

❺ Repeat with remaining ingredients for a second pizza. (The 2 pizzas may be prepared simultaneously if you are careful in placing the pizzas at opposite corners of your pizza stone.)

Grilled Eggplant Cheeseless Pizza

Grilled Eggplant

3 to 4 small Japanese eggplants, sliced lengthwise $^1/_8$ inch thick

2 tablespoons olive oil

$^1/_2$ teaspoon soy sauce

$^1/_4$ teaspoon cumin

Pinch cayenne pepper

For the Pizza

1 recipe Basic or Honey-Wheat Pizza Dough (page 7)

Cornmeal, semolina or flour for handling

2 tablespoons extra virgin olive oil

$^2/_3$ cup red onion, sliced into $^1/_8$-inch-thick half-rings

2 tablespoons chopped fresh cilantro

4 cups $^1/_4$-inch strips raw spinach

6 oil-packed sun-dried tomatoes, drained and cut into $^1/_8$-inch strips

Extra virgin olive oil (accompaniment)

Good vinegar, such as aged red wine vinegar or balsamic vinegar (accompaniment)

The original version of this pizza was made with chopped radicchio; it didn't get us the raves we like to hear. So we switched to spinach with sun-dried tomatoes, and our customers were thrilled. Thus we learned an important lesson: Trust your instincts and go with what tastes good.

To make Grilled Eggplant:

1 Prepare a hot grill.

2 Combine olive oil, soy sauce and spices. Use a pastry brush to lightly coat the slices of eggplant on both sides. Take care not to saturate the eggplant with oil. Discard outside skin-covered slices.

3 Grill the eggplant 2 to 3 minutes per side. Remove from grill and set aside in the refrigerator.

To make the pizza:

4 Place the pizza stone in the center of the oven and preheat to 500°F for one hour before cooking pizzas.

See page 9 for directions for handling and shaping the doughs.

5 Brush 1 tablespoon olive oil over the surface of the prepared pizza dough. Distribute half the onions over the oiled surface, within the rim.

6 Form a complete layer of grilled eggplant over the onions, overlapping slightly—leave no bare spots.

7 Transfer the pizza to the oven; bake until the crust is crisp and golden and the cheese at the center is bubbly, 7 to 8 minutes.

8 Slice the pizza, top with the cilantro, and then top with the 2 cups spinach. Place 18 to 20 strips sun-dried tomato over the spinach. Serve with oil and vinegar on the side. (Herb-Mustard Vinaigrette [page 83] may be substituted for oil and vinegar.)

9 Repeat with remaining ingredients for a second pizza. (The 2 pizzas may be prepared simultaneously if you are careful in placing the pizzas at opposite corners of your pizza stone.)

Eggplant Parmesan Pizza

Marinara Sauce

1 tablespoon extra virgin
    olive oil
2 teaspoons minced fresh garlic
1 tablespoon finely
    chopped onion
2 roma (plum) tomatoes,
    $1/2$-inch dice
1 tablespoon dry red wine
    (for example, Chianti)
1 teaspoon chopped
    fresh oregano leaves
    (or $1/2$ teaspoon dried)
1 tablespoon chopped
    fresh basil leaves
    (or $1/2$ teaspoon dried)
$1/2$ teaspoon salt
Pinch freshly ground
    black pepper
1 tablespoon tomato paste

Eggplant Parmesan

$1/2$ eggplant, cut into
    $1/2$-inch-thick round slices
1 large egg, well beaten
About 2 cups seasoned
    bread crumbs
$1/3$ cup olive oil
$1/4$ cup grated parmesan cheese

*This pizza is a perfect
example of what we do.
We noticed the long
standing popularity of
eggplant parmesan, which
we served at our
restaurant. A light bulb
flashed on in our minds.
We experimented, tasted
the outcome and loved it.*

For the Pizza

1 recipe Basic Pizza Dough
    (page 7)
Cornmeal, semolina or
    flour for handling
2 cups shredded mozzarella
    cheese
$1/2$ cup thinly sliced white
    mushrooms
$1/4$ cup grated parmesan cheese
4 teaspoons chopped fresh
    Italian parsley

To make Marinara Sauce:

❶ Cook the garlic and onions, stirring occasionally, in olive oil in a nonstick pan over medium heat for 1 to 2 minutes. Add the remainder of the sauce ingredients except tomato paste; reduce heat and cook, stirring frequently, until the tomato juices evaporate, about 10 minutes. Stir in tomato paste and cook for 2 minutes. Remove from heat; set aside.

To make Eggplant Parmesan:

❷ Coat eggplant slices with beaten egg; stand the slices on edge to drain. Thoroughly coat the eggplant with bread crumbs; set aside. (Discard any unused bread crumbs.)

❸ Heat oil in a large skillet until it just begins to smoke. Carefully place the breaded eggplant in the oil, rotating the pan to ensure even browning. Check the eggplant after 2 to 3 minutes; when lightly browned, use fork and tongs to carefully turn the slices over. Sprinkle a small amount of parmesan on each of the cooked eggplant surfaces.

4 When the second side is done (about 2 minutes) transfer the slices, cheese side down, to a smooth surface, such as a plate or sheet pan. Sprinkle the remainder of the parmesan over the hot surfaces of the eggplant; set aside. Slice in half when cool.

To make the pizza:

5 Place the pizza stone in the center of the oven and preheat to 500°F for one hour before cooking the pizzas.

See page 9 for directions for handling and shaping the doughs.

6 Use a large spoon to spread a generous ¼ cup Marinara Sauce over the surface of the prepared pizza dough, within the rim. Cover the sauce with ¾ cup mozzarella and half the mushrooms.

7 Place slices of eggplant over the cheese (6 to 7 half-slices); do not overlap. Sprinkle ¼ cup mozzarella over the eggplant followed by 2 tablespoons parmesan.

8 Transfer the pizza to the oven; bake until the crust is crisp and golden and the cheese at the center is bubbly, 9 to 10 minutes. When the pizza is fully cooked, carefully remove from the oven and sprinkle 2 teaspoons chopped parsley over the hot, cheesy surface. Slice and serve.

9 Repeat with remaining ingredients for a second pizza. (The 2 pizzas may be prepared simultaneously if you are careful in placing the pizzas at opposite corners of your pizza stone.)

Vegetarian Pizza with Broccoli

MAKES 2 9-INCH PIZZAS

Tomato Sauce

1 tablespoon extra virgin
   olive oil
2 teaspoons minced fresh garlic
2 roma (plum) tomatoes, diced
   $1/2$ inch (about 1 cup)
1 teaspoon chopped
   fresh oregano leaves
   (or $1/2$ teaspoon dried)
1 tablespoon chopped
   fresh basil leaves
   (or $1/2$ tablespoon dried)
$1/2$ teaspoon salt
Pinch freshly ground black
   pepper
1 tablespoon tomato paste

Grilled Eggplant

2 to 3 small Japanese eggplants,
   sliced lengthwise $1/8$ inch
   thick
2 tablespoons olive oil
$1/4$ teaspoon cumin
Pinch cayenne pepper
$1/2$ teaspoon soy sauce

For the Pizza:

1 recipe Honey-Wheat Pizza
   Dough (page 7)

Cornmeal, semolina or
   flour for handling
$1^1/2$ cups shredded
   mozzarella cheese
$1/2$ cup thinly sliced white
   mushrooms
$1/2$ cup thinly sliced red onion
6 oil-packed sun-dried tomatoes,
   drained and sliced into
   $1/8$-inch strips
2 cups blanched, drained
   broccoli florets, 1 inch
   across
2 teaspoons chopped
   fresh oregano leaves
   (or 1 teaspoon dried)

To make Tomato Sauce:

❶ Cook the garlic in olive oil in a nonstick pan over medium heat, stirring, for 1 to 2 minutes. Add the remainder of the sauce ingredients except tomato paste; reduce heat and cook, stirring frequently until the tomato juices evaporate, about 10 minutes. Stir in tomato paste and cook for two minutes. Remove from heat; set aside.

To make Grilled Eggplant:

2 Prepare a hot grill.

3 Combine olive oil, soy sauce and spices. Use a pastry brush to lightly coat the slices of eggplant on both sides. Take care not to saturate the eggplant with oil. Discard outside, skin-covered slices.

4 Grill the eggplant 2 to 3 minutes per side. Remove from grill and set aside in the refrigerator.

To make the pizza:

5 Place the pizza stone in the center of the oven and preheat to 500°F for one hour before cooking the pizzas.

See page 9 for directions for handling and shaping the doughs.

6 Use a large spoon to spread 3 tablespoons of tomato sauce evenly over the surface of the prepared dough, within the rim. Place 3 to 4 slices of eggplant over the sauce—do not overlap. Cover the eggplant with ³/₄ cup mozzarella cheese.

7 Distribute ¼ cup each sliced mushrooms and onions over the cheese. Sprinkle approximately 20 strips sun-dried tomato over the onions. Place about 18 broccoli florets over the other toppings.

8 Transfer the pizza to the oven; bake until the crust is crisp and golden and the cheese at the center is bubbly, 8 to 10 minutes.

9 When the pizza is cooked, remove from the oven and sprinkle 1 teaspoon chopped oregano over the top of the cooked pizza.

10 Repeat with remaining ingredients for a second pizza. (The 2 pizzas may be prepared simultaneously if you are careful in placing the pizzas at opposite corners of your pizza stone.)

Mixed Grill Vegetarian Pizza

MAKES 2 9-INCH PIZZAS

This pizza is the response to our customers' increasing requests for more vegetarian items on our menu. It also responds to America's growing love affair with flavors that come from the grill. In this pizza everything is grilled—even the sauce.

Grilled Vegetables and Sauce

1 tablespoon soy sauce
$1/4$ cup olive oil
2 to 3 Japanese eggplants, sliced lengthwise $1/8$ inch thick
$1/2$ medium zucchini, sliced lengthwise $1/8$ inch thick
$1/2$ red bell pepper, seeds, veins and stem removed
$1/2$ yellow bell pepper, seeds, veins and stem removed
1 small red onion, cut into $1/2$-inch rings (keep rings intact)
2 whole roma (plum) tomatoes
1 to 2 tablespoons extra virgin olive oil
Salt and pepper to taste

For the Pizza

1 recipe Basic Pizza Dough or Honey-Wheat Pizza Dough (page 7)
Cornmeal, semolina or flour for handling
$1^{1}/2$ cups shredded mozzarella cheese
12 very thin slices smoked mozzarella cheese (4 x 1-inch)

To make Grilled Vegetables and Sauce:

❶ Prepare a hot grill.

❷ Combine soy sauce and $1/4$ cup olive oil. Use a pastry brush to lightly coat the vegetables on all surfaces, being careful not to saturate the eggplant.

❸ Grill the vegetables: 2 to 3 minutes per side for the zucchini and eggplant; 5 to 6 minutes per side for the peppers and onions; 20 to 30 minutes for the tomatoes—until they are blackened on all sides. Set aside in the refrigerator.

❹ When the tomatoes have cooled, cut off the tops to remove and discard the core. Combine the tomatoes, accumulated juices and extra virgin olive oil in a food processor. Process until smooth and emulsified. Season with salt and pepper to taste. Set aside in the refrigerator until ready to assemble pizzas.

To make the pizza:

5 Place the pizza stone on the center of the oven and preheat to 500°F for one hour before cooking the pizza.

See page 9 for directions for handling and shaping the doughs.

6 Use a large spoon to spread ¼ cup of the grilled roma tomato sauce evenly over the crust, up to the rim. Spread ¾ cup (per pizza) of shredded mozzarella over the sauce.

7 Cut the grilled vegetables into strips or other managcable pieces. Place the vegetables over the cheese in successive layers reserving half the vegetables for the second pizza. Don't overcrowd—keep the toppings relatively light; you should still be able to see glimpses of cheese and all vegetables when finished. Place strips of smoked mozzarella over the vegetables.

8 Transfer the pizzas to the oven; bake until the crust is golden and the cheese at the center is hot and bubbly, 8 to 10 minutes. When cooked, remove the pizza from the oven; slice and serve.

9 Repeat with remaining ingredients for a second pizza. (The 2 pizzas may be prepared simultaneously if you are careful in placing the pizzas at opposite corners of your pizza stone.)

Novelty
Pizzas

Eggs Benedict Pizza

This recipe provides a new "twist" on pizza (pun intended) while displaying the versatility of the California Pizza.

Hollandaise Sauce
12 tablespoons (1$^1/_2$ sticks)
   unsalted butter
3 egg yolks
1 tablespoon cold water
1$^1/_2$ tablespoons freshly
   squeezed lemon juice
$^1/_8$ teaspoon cayenne pepper
Pinch ground white pepper
Salt to taste

For the Pizza
1 recipe Basic Pizza Dough
   (page 7)
Cornmeal, semolina or
   flour for handling
1 cup shredded mozzarella
   cheese
12 large spinach leaves,
   blanched and wrung dry
4 round slices Canadian-style
   bacon
4 poached or coddled eggs,
   cooked soft and drained of
   excess water

To make Hollandaise Sauce:

❶ Melt butter in a small saucepan over low heat; keep warm.

❷ Combine egg yolks, cold water and lemon juice in a stainless steel bowl; whisk to blend thoroughly.

❸ Place the bowl over saucepan of simmering water (do not allow the water to touch the bottom of the bowl). Whip constantly until the eggs become frothy and turn from dark yellow to light yellow.

❹ Remove from heat. Wrap a damp towel around the bottom of the bowl to help stabilize it. Slowly add the hot butter while whipping vigorously and constantly. When all the butter has been incorporated, season the sauce to taste with pepper and salt. Set aside, warm for immediate use.

Top *Eggs Benedict Pizza;*
Bottom *Pear-Brie Calzone
(recipe on next page)*

To make the pizza:

5 Place the pizza stone in the center of the oven and preheat to 500°F for one hour before cooking the pizzas.

See page 9 for directions for handling and shaping the doughs.

After you have stretched the dough, twist it to form a figure "8."

6 Fill each side of the "8" with ¼ cup mozzarella. Unfold half the blanched spinach leaves and press them down over the cheese, covering it and beginning to form 2 distinct cups. Press rounds of Canadian-style bacon into the 2 cups.

7 Transfer the pizza to the oven; bake until the dough is browned all over, 8 to 10 minutes. Mean-while cook and drain the eggs.

8 Remove the cooked pizza from the oven; place the eggs into the bacon "cups." Top the eggs with Hollandaise Sauce and serve immediately with knife and fork.

9 Repeat with remaining ingredients for a second pizza. (The 2 pizzas may be prepared simultaneously if you are careful in placing the pizzas at opposite corners of your pizza stone.)

Pear-Brie Calzone

MAKES 2 CALZONES

Caramelized Pears

1½ tablespoons unsalted butter
1 pound whole pears, peeled, cored and sliced ⅛ inch thick
Pinch ground cinnamon
¼ teaspoon vanilla extract
¼ teaspoon almond extract
1 tablespoon granulated sugar

This is our California-style version of French Toast. This calzone vividly demonstrates the versatility of our pizza dough. Try this one for Sunday brunch; it will open your eyes to infinite possibilities.

For the Calzone

1½ quarts vegetable oil for deep frying
1 recipe Basic Pizza Dough (page 7)
Cornmeal, semolina or flour for handling
1 whole egg beaten with 1 teaspoon cold water
¼ cup sliced almonds
¼ pound brie, cut into ½-inch cubes
¼ cup powdered sugar
½ cup warm pure maple syrup

To make Caramelized Pears:

1 Cook the pears in butter over high heat, stirring, until they begin to brown, 4 to 5 minutes. Add remaining ingredients; reduce heat to medium and continue to cook until pears are uniformly caramelized brown. Cool.

To make the calzone:

2 Heat deep-frying oil to 375°F (just short of smoking temperature).

See page 9 for directions for handling and shaping the doughs.

However, when making calzones it is not necessary or desirable to form a lip. Instead, use a rolling pin or your hands to form a 9- to 10-inch flat circle. Place the dough on a square of aluminum foil.

3 Brush the egg-and-water mixture in a 1-inch stripe along the edge of half the dough (this acts as the "glue" to seal the calzone closed).

4 Spread half the pears over the center of the dough. Keep this and all other fillings 1½ inches away from the edges. Cover the pears with half the sliced almonds and half the brie. Carefully sprinkle half the powdered sugar over the filling, staying clean of the edges.

5 Pull the non-egg-coated side of the dough over the top of the filling and press the edges of the dough together with fingers or a spoon to form a complete seal. If desired, you can use a pizza wheel to trim of excess uneven edges.

6 Immerse the calzone into the deep-frying oil being extremely careful to avoid splashing hot oil on yourself. After 2 minutes, use 2 wooden spoons or paddles to turn the calzone over in the oil to allow the other side to brown. After 2 minutes more, carefully remove the calzone from the oil using a poaching tool or some other perforated, stable tool.

7 Drain the calzone on paper towels briefly and transfer it to a serving plate. Pour ¼ cup warm maple syrup around the calzone, on the plate. Dust with powdered sugar and serve with knife and fork.

8 Repeat with remaining ingredients for a second calzone.

Zabaglione Pizzas

*"You put everything else on a pizza, why not dessert?"
We can't remember how many times we were asked that question, but eventually we got the message and began experimenting with various recipes.
We probably could have done anything from banana cream pie to chocolate pudding pizza, but perfecting Zabaglione truly proved we could—and did—do everything on a pizza from A to Z.*

Mascarpone Zabaglione

2 jumbo eggs (yolks only)
1$^{1}/_{2}$ tablespoons plus 2 teaspoons granulated sugar
2 teaspoons dry Italian marsala wine
$^{1}/_{2}$ cup (4$^{1}/_{2}$ ounces) mascarpone (a sweet Italian cream cheese), at room temperature
$^{1}/_{4}$ cup heavy cream
$^{1}/_{4}$ teaspoon vanilla extract

Caramelized Apple

1 medium Granny Smith apple, peeled, cored, and sliced $^{1}/_{8}$ inch thick
1 tablespoon unsalted butter
$^{1}/_{4}$ teaspoon vanilla extract
1 tablespoon granulated sugar
Small pinch cinnamon
$^{1}/_{4}$ teaspoon lemon juice
2 tablespoons heavy cream

For the Pizzas

2 recipes Basic Pizza Dough (very puffy, well proofed, page 7)
1 cup granulated sugar
Flour for handling
Other toppings

Almost any fruit may be substituted for the Caramelized Apples in this recipe: sliced berries or sliced bananas may be used without precooking. Other fruits such as peaches or apricots may require precooking if they contain a great deal of water or if softening is desired.

To make Mascarpone Zabaglione:

❶ Combine egg yolks, 1$^{1}/_{2}$ tablespoons sugar and marsala in a stainless steel bowl; beat with a whisk to blend well. Place the bowl over a saucepan of simmering water (do not allow water to touch the bottom of the bowl). Whip until the mixture triples in volume, 3 to 5 minutes. Cover and refrigerate until well chilled.

❷ In another bowl beat cream, vanilla and 2 teaspoons sugar together to form soft peaks. Gently fold the whipped cream into the softened mascarpone cheese.

3 Gently fold the chilled egg mixture into the cheese and cream. Cover and set aside in the refrigerator.

To make Caramelized Apple:

4 Cook the apple slices in butter over high heat, stirring, until they begin to brown, 5 minutes. Add vanilla, cinnamon, lemon juice and sugar. Reduce heat to medium and cook until apple slices are caramel brown, stirring frequently.

5 Add cream and use a rubber spatula to deglaze the pan with the cream. Continue cooking until the cream becomes a coating on the apple slices; cool.

To make the pizza:

6 Place the pizza stone in the center of the oven and preheat to 500°F for one hour before cooking the pizzas.

See page 9 for directions for handling and shaping the doughs.

However, these pizzas are made intentionally smaller and thicker than our regular pizzas. Also, we recommend that you cook these pizzas on aluminum foil to keep juices, cheese and sugar from getting on your pizza stone.

7 Remove the well-proofed, puffy dough from the dish and press the sticky upper surface into a plate of granulated sugar. Carefully remove the dough from the sugar, placing the other side down on a liberally floured smooth surface. Gently form a large puffy rim around the edge of the dough. The dough should be about 6 inches in diameter (even though it is the same amount of dough we usually stretch to 9 inches).

8 Carefully transfer the dough to a floured sheet of aluminum foil. Re-form the edges of the rim to prevent Zabaglione from running out. Pour 2 to 3 tablespoons of Zabaglione into the center of the prepared dough. Place approximately 2 tablespoons of fruit over the sauce. Sprinkle 2 to 3 teaspoons sugar over the entire surface including edges.

9 Transfer the pizza, foil and all, to the pizza stone in the oven. Cook 7 to 8 minutes; crust should be browned and sparkling, and the exposed Zabaglione should be caramelized like a crème brûlée surface. Give the foil a light shake to ensure that the custard has set.

10 Carefully remove the pizza and foil from the oven. Allow the pizza to sit for 1 to 2 minutes before removing foil. Transfer the pizza to a serving plate. Slice and serve.

11 Repeat with remaining ingredients for three more pizzas (people generally eat a lot of these). Several pizzas may be prepared simultaneously if so desired.

Pasta, Soups, Salads and Sides

Broccoli and Sun-Dried Tomato Fusilli

Makes 4 to 6 servings

Rick and his wife Esther and Larry and his wife Joni often cooked together in their homes. A favorite dish became their creation of fusilli pasta—the corkscrew-shaped type— topped with broccoli and sun-dried tomatoes. They liked it so much they decided to add it to California Pizza Kitchen's menu. It instantly became a favorite.

1 pound dry fusilli pasta
  (or 2 pounds fresh)
$^1/_2$ cup extra virgin olive oil
1 teaspoon kosher salt
$^1/_4$ cup chopped fresh garlic
2 tablespoons chopped
  fresh thyme leaves
Approximately 12 oil-packed
  sun-dried tomatoes,
  drained and sliced into
  thin strips
1 quart blanched broccoli
  florets, drained bite-size
1$^1/_4$ cups grated parmesan
  cheese ($^1/_4$ cup reserved
  for garnish)

❶ Bring a large pot of salted water to a boil. Cook pasta until al dente, 8 to 10 minutes for dry pasta or 3 minutes for fresh. Pasta may be cooked slightly ahead of time, rinsed and oiled and then "flashed" (reheated) in boiling water to coincide with the finishing of the sauce/topping.

❷ Heat olive oil in a large non-stick frying pan over high heat. Add salt and garlic; when the garlic just begins to brown, add thyme and sun-dried tomatoes. Toss and add broccoli. When broccoli is heated through, add drained pasta (if pan is not large enough to accommodate this large load, proceed quickly in a large mixing bowl, while ingredients are still quite hot). Add 1 cup parmesan to the pan, sprinkling and tossing/stirring to mix.

❸ Remove from heat; serve the pasta in warm bowls with a fresh dusting of parmesan cheese.

Note: *Fresh diced tomatoes can be added along with the broccoli if so desired, as pictured on page 81.*

Top *Broccoli and Sun-Dried Tomato Fusilli;* **Bottom** *Chicken Tequila Fettucine (recipe on next page)*

Chicken Tequila Fettucine

Recipes evolve on their own. Early on, we put a shot of tequila in each dish. The bottle was kept over the range. Then one day it heated up, accidentally tipped and burst into flames. After that, we started putting the tequila right in the sauce. Too much of this one and you really will end up south of the border—or under the table.

1 pound dry spinach fettucine (or 2 pounds fresh)
$^1/_2$ cup chopped fresh cilantro (2 tablespoons reserved for garnish/finish)
2 tablespoons minced fresh garlic
2 tablespoons minced jalapeño pepper (seeds and veins may be eliminated if milder flavor is desired)

3 tablespoons unsalted butter (reserve 1 tablespoon per sauté)
$^1/_2$ cup chicken stock (preferably homemade)
2 tablespoons gold tequila
2 tablespoons freshly squeezed lime juice
3 tablespoons soy sauce
$1^1/_4$ pounds chicken breast, diced $^3/_4$ inch
$^1/_4$ medium red onion, thinly sliced
$^1/_2$ medium red bell pepper, thinly sliced
$^1/_2$ medium yellow bell pepper, thinly sliced
$^1/_2$ medium green bell pepper, thinly sliced
$1^1/_2$ cups heavy cream

❶ Prepare rapidly boiling, salted water to cook pasta; cook until al dente, 8 to 10 minutes for dry pasta, approximately 3 minutes for fresh. Pasta may be cooked slightly ahead of time, rinsed and oiled and then "flashed" (reheated) in boiling water or cooked to coincide with the finishing of the sauce/topping.

❷ Cook $^1/_3$ cup cilantro, garlic and jalapeño in 2 tablespoons butter over medium heat for 4 to 5 minutes. Add stock, tequila and lime juice. Bring the mixture to a boil and cook until reduced to a pastelike consistency; set aside.

❸ Pour soy sauce over diced chicken; set aside for 5 minutes. Meanwhile cook onion and peppers, stirring occasionally, with remaining butter over medium heat. When the vegetables have wilted (become limp), add chicken and soy sauce; toss and add reserved tequila/lime paste and cream.

❹ Bring the sauce to a boil; boil gently until chicken is cooked through and sauce is thick (about 3 minutes). When sauce is done, toss with well-drained spinach fettucine and reserved cilantro.

❺ Serve family style or transfer to serving dishes, evenly distributing chicken and vegetables.

Chopped Salad with Herb-Mustard Vinaigrette

Makes 4 entree servings or 8 appetizer servings

It takes some work, but this salad proved a real timesaver for us. Why? Because even though we had a restaurant that served a variety of great salads, we still found ourselves wandering up the street occasionally to indulge in an Italian-style chopped salad. So we decided to save ourselves the trip and create our own.

Herb-Mustard Vinaigrette

1 teaspoon minced fresh garlic

2 teaspoons minced fresh shallot

2 tablespoons Dijon mustard

$1^{1}/_{2}$ teaspoons dried oregano

2 teaspoons dried parsley

$^{1}/_{2}$ teaspoon ground black pepper

$^{1}/_{4}$ teaspoon kosher salt

$^{1}/_{4}$ cup red wine vinegar

$1^{1}/_{3}$ cups pure, mild-flavored olive oil

3 tablespoons grated parmesan cheese

Salad

$^{1}/_{2}$ head iceberg lettuce, cleaned, trimmed and chopped into $^{1}/_{8}$-inch-wide strips

$^{1}/_{2}$ head romaine lettuce, cleaned trimmed and chopped into $^{1}/_{8}$-inch-wide strips

12 large leaves basil, chopped into $^{1}/_{16}$-inch-wide strips

2 cups ($^{1}/_{3}$ pound) dry Italian salami, cut into thin strips

3 cups ($^{2}/_{3}$ pound) shredded mozzarella cheese

1 cup chopped garbanzo beans

4 cups (2 pounds) ripe tomatoes, diced $^{1}/_{2}$ inch

3 cups (1 pound) turkey breast, diced $^{1}/_{2}$ inch

2 tablespoons chopped scallions, $^{1}/_{4}$-inch pieces

To make the dressing:

❶ Process all ingredients except oil and parmesan using a hand-held, propeller-blade type mixer (or use a whisk in a small bowl). Slowly blend in oil. When all oil has been incorporated, stir in parmesan. Set aside in the refrigerator.

To make the salad:

❷ Toss first 6 ingredients and dressing together in a large mixing bowl. Transfer the salads to chilled salad plates. Surround each serving with a ring of diced tomatoes and top with diced turkey breast. Garnish with chopped scallions.

Note: *If so desired, all ingredients can be tossed together instead of being composed on the plate as described earlier.*

Romaine-Watercress Salad with Balsamic-Basil Vinaigrette

MAKES 4 ENTRÉE SERVINGS OR 8 APPETIZER SERVINGS

Balsamic-Basil Vinaigrette
6 to 8 large fresh basil leaves
6 tablespoons balsamic vinegar
$1/4$ pound Gorgonzola cheese, crumbled
$3/4$ cup pure, mild-flavored olive oil

Romaine-Watercress Salad
1 head ($1^1/2$ pounds) romaine lettuce, cleaned, cored and cut into 1-inch bite-size squares
1 bunch watercress, cleaned and cut into bite-size lengths
8 ounces Gorgonzola cheese, crumbled
2 cups walnuts, shelled halves

Originally, we served this salad with a thin balsamic vinaigrette, but customers kept asking for more gorgonzola and suggested the dressing was a bit too vinegary for their taste. Consequently, we added gorgonzola to the dressing itself, satisfying both requests.

To make the dressing:
❶ Process all ingredients except oil using a hand-held, propeller-blade type mixer (or use a whisk in a small bowl). Slowly blend in oil; set aside in the refrigerator.

To make the salad:
❷ Combine the greens in a large mixing bowl. Add dressing and toss to coat all leaves. Transfer the dressed greens to chilled serving plates. Top each serving with equal amounts of crumbled Gorgonzola cheese and walnuts.

Top *Chopped Salad with Herb-Mustard Vinaigrette (recipe on previous page);* **Bottom** *Romaine-Watercress Salad with Balsamic-Basil Vinaigrette.*

Potato-Leek Soup

For a long time, salud was the only starter we offered. Then we opened in Chicago and we were overwhelmed with requests for soup. In response we began offering the Sedona White Corn Tortilla soup, which was an instant hit. Soon after, we introduced Potato Leek to provide another choice. Inspired by famous California chef John Sedlar's idea for combining two soups, Larry tried it with our own to create Two-in-a-bowl Soup. It was another hit.

$^1/_2$ **pound leeks (cleancd, trimmed and sliced $^1/_4$ inch; white part only)**

1 **pound russet potatoes, peeled, dried and cut into $^1/_2$-inch chunks**

3 **cups water**

2 **teaspoons kosher salt**

1 **bay leaf**

$^3/_4$ **teaspoon dried oregano**

$^3/_4$ **teaspoon dried thyme**

$^1/_2$ **teaspoon ground white pepper**

1$^1/_2$ **tablespoons extra virgin olive oil**

1 **teaspoon soy sauce**

1$^1/_3$ **cups chicken stock (preferably homemade)**

$^1/_2$ **cup heavy cream**

1$^1/_2$ **cups half-and-half**

2 **tablespoons chopped scallion greens (optional garnish)**

To make the soup:

❶ Place half the leeks and all the potatoes, water, salt, herbs and spices in a 3-quart pot over medium heat. While the potatoes are cooking, cook the remaining leeks in olive oil in a separate pan over medium heat for 10 to 15 minutes, stirring frequently. Add soy sauce to leeks after they have begun to caramelize; they should not be crispy or black. Continue cooking, gently, until the leeks are a uniform caramel color.

❷ Add the stock to the leek pan and carefully pour leeks and stock into the potato pot. Use a rubber spatula to recover all pan drippings and add them to the potatoes.

❸ When the potatoes are soft and crumbly, remove the pot from the burner; remove and discard bay leaf and process the soup to a coarse puree. Return the soup to the pot, whisk in cream and half-and-half. Bring the soup to a gentle boil and remove from heat.

❹ Soup may be served at once, garnished with chopped scallion greens or olives; or may be thoroughly chilled and served as vichyssoise.

Two-in-a-bowl Soup featuring Potato-Leek Soup and Sedona White Corn Tortilla Soup (recipe on next page)

Sedona White Corn Tortilla Soup

3 tablespoons olive oil
1^1/$_2$ seven-inch corn tortillas,
    cut into 1-inch squares
1^1/$_2$ tablespoons minced
    fresh garlic
2 tablespoons minced
    white onion
1^1/$_2$ teaspoons minced
    jalapeño pepper
1 pound white corn kernels
1^1/$_2$ pounds chopped, ripe
    red tomatoes
^{1}/$_3$ cup tomato paste
2^1/$_2$ teaspoons ground cumin
1 tablespoon kosher salt
^{1}/$_8$ teaspoon ground white
    pepper
^{1}/$_2$ teaspoon chili powder
1^1/$_2$ cups water
1 quart chicken stock
    (preferably homemade)
24 blue corn tortilla chips
    (optional garnish)
2 cups shredded sharp cheddar
    (optional garnish)
^{1}/$_2$ cup chopped fresh cilantro
    (optional garnish)

1 Over medium-high heat, fry tortilla squares in olive oil until they begin to crisp and turn a golden yellow. Add garlic, onion and jalapeño; cook 1 to 2 minutes, until onion becomes translucent. Add half the corn along with all other ingredients (except garnishes), reserving other half of corn to be added at the end. Bring the soup to a low, even boil. Boil for 5 minutes.

2 Remove soup from heat. Use a hand-held propeller blade processor or food processor to process in batches to the consistency of a course puree.

3 Return the soup to the burner and add the reserved corn. Bring the soup to a boil once again being extremely careful to avoid scorching or burning. Serve, garnished with blue corn tortilla chips, cilantro and sharp cheddar cheese.

Sweet Corn Tamalitos

10 to 12 large dried corn husks
(available in Hispanic and/or
gourmet markets)
1 pound sweet white corn kernels
2 tablespoons unsalted butter
$^1/_4$ cup heavy cream
$^1/_2$ cup masa de maiz
(fine cornmeal)
$^1/_2$ teaspoon baking powder
$^1/_4$ teaspoon salt
$^1/_8$ teaspoon ground white pepper
1 tablespoon sugar
$^1/_2$ teaspoon minced jalapeño
pepper
$^1/_2$ cup finely shredded white
sharp cheddar cheese
1 to 2 cups boiling water
$^1/_2$ cup sour cream
(suggested accompaniment)

1 Soak corn husks in warm water to soften.

2 Combine next 9 ingredients in a nonstick pot over low heat; mix thoroughly while heating through. When mixture is steaming hot, transfer to the work bowl of a food processor. Process for about 1 minute stopping occasionally to scrape down the sides of the container. Add cheese and mix through. Transfer to a bowl for easy handling.

3 Remove the husks from their soaking water and drain on a clean towel.

4 Place about 3 tablespoons of the tamale mixture in the center of each corn husk. Fold the edges of the husk over the tamale mixture, sealing it inside the husk. (First overlap the sides; then fold the ends under.) Place the folded tamalitos in a steamer. Pour boiling water into the bottom section to below the steamer insert. Steam for 75 minutes. Be sure to add more water to the steamer if necessary.

5 When the tamalitos are cooked, remove them from the oven and let them rest for 10 minutes on a covered plate before serving. Serve with sour cream.

Again, take a tip from your own eating habits. Rick suggested trying this after he found himself ordering it in a restaurant on a regular basis. Given our success with southwestern cuisine, it seemed like a natural.

Photography Credits

Chicken Dijon Pizza

Page 17, Aletha Soule Dijon Melange plate from **Vanderbilt & Co.**, Palo Alto, CA.

Rosemary Chicken and Potato Pizza

Page 18, Anagram hand-painted plate from **Tesoro,** Beverly Hills, CA. Le Jacquard Français Clafoutis tea towel from **French Garden Shoppe,** DelMar, CA.

Chicken Tostada Pizza

Page 21, Hilary Harris Tomato plate from **Freehand,** Los Angeles.

Santa Fe Chicken Pizza

Page 24, Chili pepper tray, iron flatware, Xochi napkin from **Tesoro.** Kristen Nelson plate and cowboy napkin ring from **New Stone Age,** Los Angeles.

Tandoori Chicken Pizza

Page 28, Aletha Soule Forest Melange plate from **Vanderbilt & CO.**

Thai Chicken Pizza

Page 31, Cyclamen plate from **Freehand.**

Peking Duck Pizza

Page 39, Le Jacquard Français Shanghai linens from **Malibu Colony Co.**

BLT Pizza

Page 41, Diner greeting cards from **The Folk Tree Collection.**

Chicken Caesar Salad Pizza

Page 43, Bill Goldsmith Amalfi plate from **Geary's,** Beverly Hills, CA. Sabre flatware from **Cinzia,** Santa Monica, CA. LeJacquard Français Tutti-Frutti tea towel from **Malibu Colony Co.**, Malibu, CA.

Hawaiian Pizza

Page 44, Cyclamen plate from **Freehand.** Throb surfing poster, photographed by Don King for Surfer Publications.

Mushroom, Pepperoni and Sausage Pizza and Goat Cheese Pizza

Page 47, Placemats and napkins from **Museum of Modern Art,** New York.

Shrimp Scampi Pizza

Page 51, Sasaki flatware, Fossilglass plate, Sferra napkins, all from **Tesoro.**

Shrimp Pesto Pizza

Page 53, David Gurmey Mermaid plate from **Freehand.**

Smoked Salmon Appetizer Pizza

Page 55, Hollywood Portraits greeting cards from **Museum of Modern Art.**

Grilled Eggplant Cheeseless Pizza

Page 61, Hilary Harris plate from **Freehand.**

Eggplant Parmesan Pizza

Page 63, Charney plate from **Tesoro.**

Mixed Grill Vegetarian Pizza

Page 67, Simoncelli plate from **Freehand.**

Eggs Benedict Pizza and Pear- Brie Calzone

Page 71, Notes and Queries wrapping paper (background) from **Zero Minus Plus,** Santa Monica, CA. Le Jacquard Français napkin from **Country Down,** Del Mar, CA. Orion flute from **La Paloma Designs,** Los Angeles. Iridescent oval plate from **Hathcoat Studios,** Colorado Springs, CO. Glass plates with gold rim from **Tizo.**

Zabaglione Pizzas

Page 75, Hathcoat round plate from **Tesoro.** Octagon Tiger plate from **Hathcoat Studios.**

Broccoli and Sun-Dried Tomato Fusilli and Chicken Tequila Fettucine

Page 81, Napkin and flatware from **Tesoro.** Sabre fork from **Cinzia.**

Romaine-Watercress Salad and Chopped Salad

Page 84, Vintage Pepsi sign from **The Folk Tree Collection.** Sabre flatware from **Cinzia.** Aletha Soule Caribe Melange plate from **Vanderbilt & Co.**

Two in a Bowl Soup

Page 87, Luna Garcia bowl and plate from **New Stone Age.** Notes and Queries wrapping paper (background) from **Noteworthy,** Los Angeles.

Sweet Corn Tamalitos

Page 89, Le Jacquard Français napkin from **Country Down.**

Index